I0759749

LEGENDS OF WARFARE

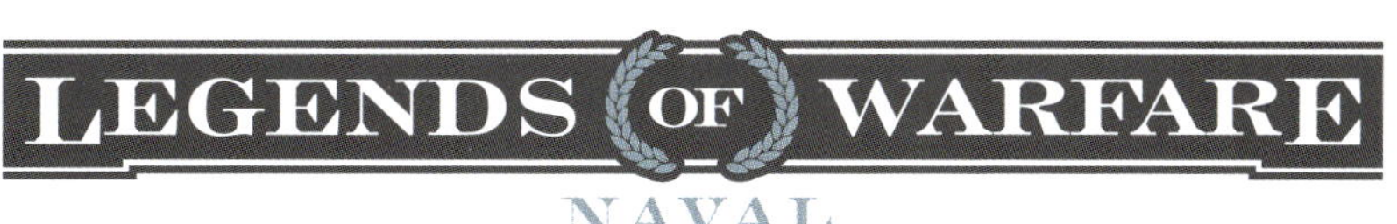

NAVAL

USS Nevada (BB-36)

US Navy Super-Dreadnought in WWI and WWII

DAVID DOYLE

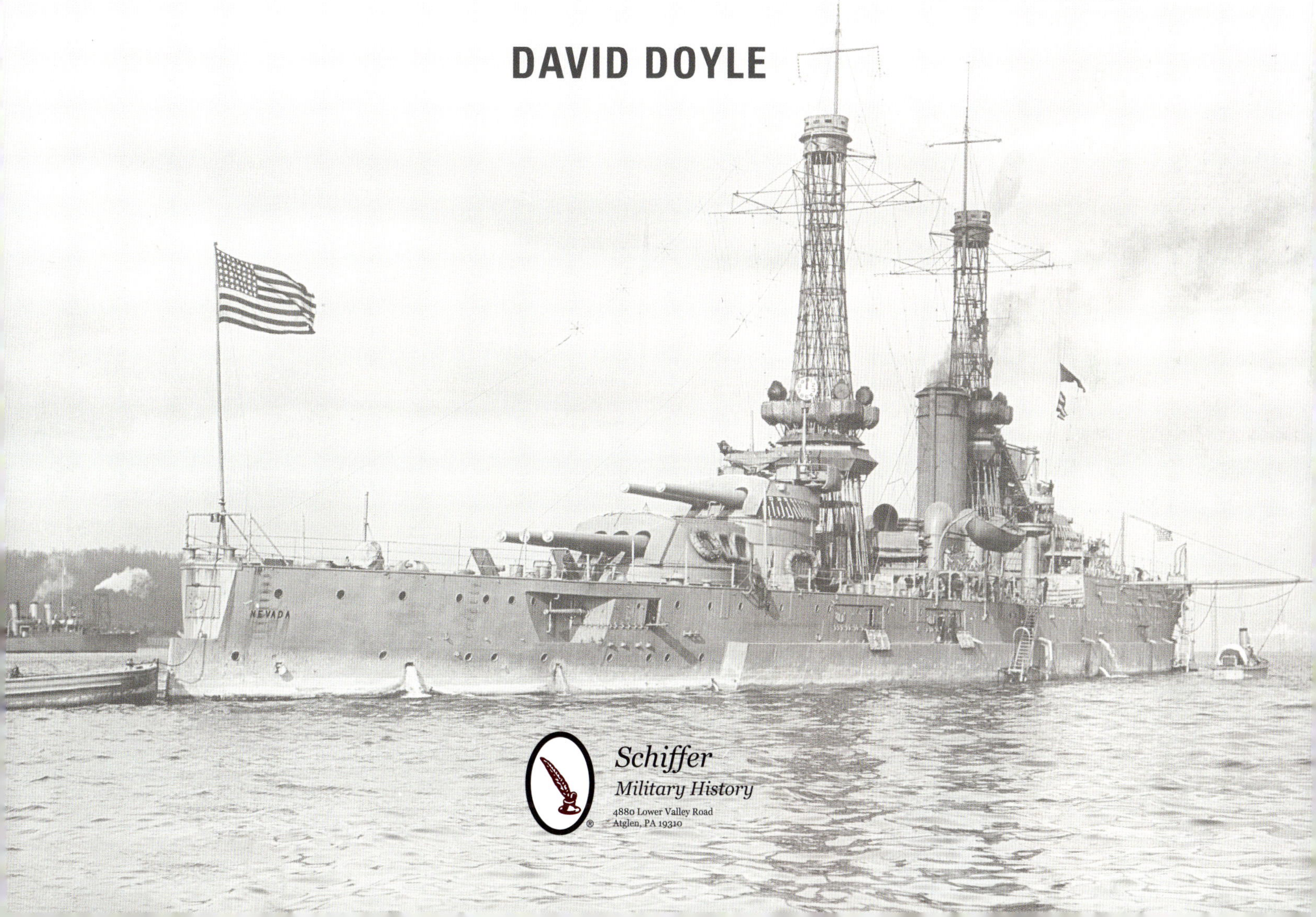

Schiffer Military History
4880 Lower Valley Road
Atglen, PA 19310

Other Schiffer books by the author
USS Indianapolis (CA-35): From Presidential Cruiser, to Delivery of the Atomic Bombs, to Tragic Sinking in WWII,
978-0-7643-6262-0

USS North Carolina (BB-55): From WWII Combat to Museum Ship,
978-0-7643-5563-9

USS Hornet (CV-8): From the Doolittle Raid and Midway to Santa Cruz,
978-0-7643-5862-3

Library of Congress Control Number: 2025939996

Designed by Alexa Harris
Type set in Impact / Univers Lt STD / Minion Pro

ISBN: 978-0-7643-7076-2

Printed in India
10 9 8 7 6 5 4 3 2 1

Published by Schiffer Publishing, Ltd.
4880 Lower Valley Road
Atglen, PA 19310
Phone: (610) 593-1777; Fax: (610) 593-2002
Email: Info@schifferbooks.com
Web: www.schifferbooks.com

Acknowledgments

While working on this book, I was blessed with the generous help of Tom Kailbourn, Scott Taylor, Tracy White, Sean Hert, Roger Torgeson, Rick Davis, James Noblin, Dana Bell, Randy Fagan of the Floating Drydock, and A. D. Baker III. As always, I could have done none of this without the support of my wonderful wife, Denise, who took notes, scanned photographs, and accompanied me on numerous research expeditions. She truly is a great blessing to me.

Contents

Introduction

The 1906 debut of HMS *Dreadnought*, with her uniform big-gun main battery and steam turbine propulsion, not only revolutionized battleship design but also rendered all prior battleships obsolete and sparked an arms race among the world powers.

Although the US Navy requested four new battleships per year from 1907 to 1914, the US Congress approved only one per year, until fiscal year 1911, when the two-ship New York class (*New York* and *Texas*) was approved, and March 1911, when the fiscal year 1912 naval appropriations act was passed by a lame-duck Congress.

On Saturday, March 4, 1911, HR 32212 was passed in the final session of the Sixty-First Congress, which had stretched into the wee hours of the morning. Included in the language of that resolution, which was the Naval Appropriation Act, were these words:

> That for the purpose of further increasing the Naval Establishment of the United States, the president is hereby authorized to have constructed two first-class battleships, each carrying as heavy armor and as powerful armament as any vessel of its class, to have the highest practicable speed and the greatest practicable radius of action, and to cost, exclusive of armor and armament, not to exceed $6,000,000 each.

This bill passed the House 59 to 17, having passed the Senate earlier in the day.

With these two ships, the US Navy put in place many characteristics that would become standard for US battleships of the dreadnought era. Chief of these was the adoption of bunker oil as fuel rather than coal. Oil contains more energy by volume than does coal, and as a result the new ships would have a greater range than their predecessors (with the same space allocated for fuel). Refueling at sea with oil was also considerably more practical than with coal, and construction of oil-fueling facilities in the remote expanses of the Pacific was far easier and less expensive than it would be for coal. Further, the labor of handling the fuel aboard ship and operating the boilers would be reduced by an estimated 80 percent, with the position of coal passer completely eliminated.

The ships also introduced a revolutionary concept in ship protection. Known as "all or nothing" armor, this approach would not only come to define successive US capital ships but also influence the design of most such vessels in other navies worldwide.

The logic behind "all or nothing" protection stemmed from the realities of long-range naval combat. At extreme distances, ships were primarily vulnerable to armor-piercing shells, since these projectiles could strike anywhere on a vessel's hull or superstructure. High-explosive rounds, effective against lightly armored targets, proved futile when faced with thick belt or deck armor. Consequently, naval designers concluded that only the heaviest armor—or none at all—was worth employing. Intermediate levels of protection served merely as bursting plates for incoming shells, adding weight without commensurate defensive value.

Utilizing this principle, the design, optimized for engagement at extreme ranges, incorporated robust protection against plunging fire—a significant threat in long-distance naval artillery duels. Two armored decks, with a combined thickness of 4.5–5 inches, ran the length of the ships' citadel. To offset the considerable weight of this armor, designers reduced the overall protected length of the vessel. This was achieved by adopting a more compact arrangement of the main battery, with four turrets instead of the five or six seen in earlier dreadnoughts.

To maintain the desired firepower within this condensed layout, the design pioneered the use of triple gun mounts in American battleships. This configuration allowed for a potent array of guns while minimizing the armored citadel's length. Further contributing to the compact design was the adoption of oil-fired boilers, fuel for which required less space than traditional coal bunkers.

The uptakes for the new ships would also be heavily armored. Although this added considerable weight high in the ship, armoring the uptakes meant preserving the ability of the ship to make steam while taking battle damage.

Sir Charles Algernon Parsons had revolutionized naval propulsion with his development of the compound steam turbine in 1887, and his adapting it for marine use in 1897. New York engineer Charles Gordon Curtis adapted some of Parson's principles to create a multistage impulse turbine that was more compact than Parson's design.

The Curtis and the Parsons turbine designs, while both harnessing the power of steam, approached the task through fundamentally different principles of fluid dynamics. The Curtis turbine, an impulse design, operated on the principle of rapid steam expansion through specially designed nozzles. This process accelerated the steam to high velocities while simultaneously reducing its pressure. The resulting high-speed, low-pressure steam jet would then impact the blades of a spinning wheel, transferring its kinetic energy into rotational motion. In contrast, the Parsons turbine utilized a reaction design. In this configuration, steam expansion occurred not only through fixed nozzles but also as it passed through the rotating blades themselves. This continuous expansion process throughout the turbine stages resulted in a different energy transfer mechanism.

While the distinction between these designs seems subtle, in practice they had profound implications for naval engineering. The different approaches to steam utilization necessitated variations in the shape and dimensions both of the nozzles and the turbine blades. These variations, in turn, affected factors such as the turbine's overall size, efficiency, and power output.

In 1897, General Electric entered an agreement with Charles Curtis to exploit his steam turbine patent (no. 566,969) for land use. Curtis directed GE's turbine development until 1900. Two years earlier, in 1895, Westinghouse had acquired rights to manufacture reaction turbines patented by English inventor Charles Parsons in 1884. Many US warships of the twentieth century were powered by either GE or Westinghouse turbines.

When *Nevada* was built, she was equipped with Curtis turbines. Because this technology was still new at the time, for comparative purposes *Nevada*'s sister ship, *Oklahoma*, was powered by triple-expansion reciprocating engines. Reciprocating engines typically are considerably more maintenance intensive than turbines but, in the early twentieth century, yielded slightly better fuel economy.

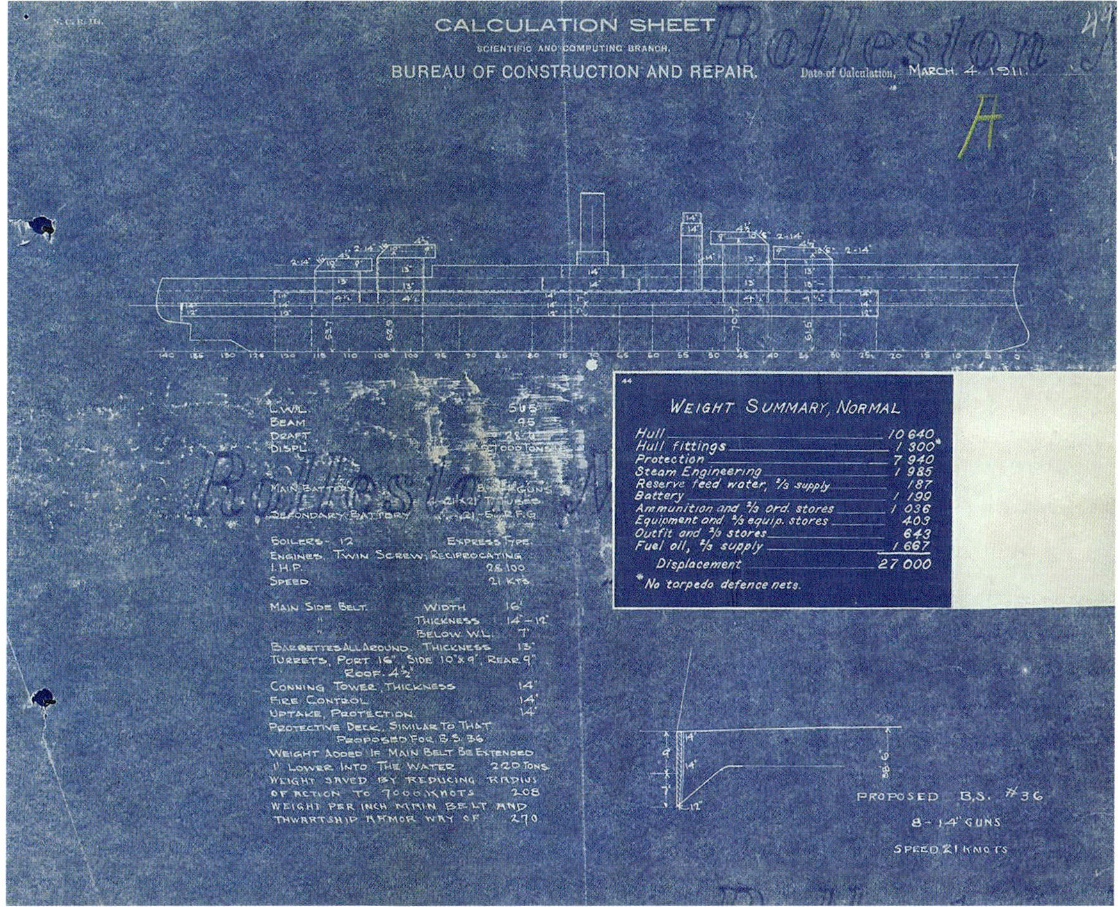

An enormous number of man-hours went into the design of warships, to ensure that the finished product would perform as planned. This calculation sheet, dated March 4, 1911, includes a schematic diagram of proposed battleship number 36 (USS *Nevada*), with armor thicknesses of various decks and structures. Also included are specifications for the ship and a summary of normal weight, totaling a displacement of 27,000 tons. *Naval History and Heritage CommandV*

CHAPTER 1

Construction and Launching

In the autumn of 1911, as the US Navy continued its steady modernization program, the process of bringing two new battleships into existence began in earnest. On October 18, Secretary of the Navy George von Lengerke Meyer approved the *Circular of Requirements for Bidders for Battleships Nos. 36 and 37, as Authorized by an Act of Congress on March 4, 1911*. This document set forth the Navy's expectations for these formidable new warships, destined to become the most-advanced and most-powerful vessels in the American fleet.

The Navy's approach to procurement allowed for a degree of innovation from commercial shipbuilders. While the circular provided detailed specifications, it also permitted bidders to propose designs "in general accordance" with the Navy's requirements. This flexibility, though rarely exercised due to the specialized nature of warship construction, demonstrated the Navy's openness to new ideas in naval architecture and engineering.

The timeline for construction was ambitious, with builders given just three years to complete each vessel. To ensure timely delivery, the Navy included provisions for substantial financial penalties for each day a ship was delayed beyond the contracted completion date.

In an era when naval supremacy was synonymous with national power, the construction of these battleships was a matter of utmost importance. The Navy allowed potential builders a mere sixty days to respond to the circular—a remarkably brief period considering the complexity of the project. This tight schedule reflected the urgency with which the Navy viewed the expansion and modernization of its battle fleet.

The Navy's selection process was multifaceted, considering not only the cost but also each bidder's capacity to complete the contract and the anticipated quality of the finished product. On January 4, 1912, at the stroke of noon, the bids were unsealed. After careful deliberation, on January 22 the Navy awarded the contract for Battleship No. 36—soon to be named *Nevada*—to the Fore River Shipbuilding Company of Quincy, Massachusetts.

Fore River's winning bid of $5,895,000 secured them the contract, but this figure represented only the base cost of construction. It did not include the expense of armor, guns, and other equipment to be supplied by the government. By the time *Nevada* was completed, with all government-furnished materials factored in, the total cost would reach $11,518,763.13—a staggering sum for the time, equivalent to over $300 million (in 2024 dollars).

The selection of Fore River Shipbuilding Company was no coincidence. Founded in 1883 by Thomas Watson, former assistant to Alexander Graham Bell, the company had rapidly evolved from its origins in manufacturing small-ship engines. By the turn of the century, Fore River was competing for and winning significant Navy contracts.

In 1901, Watson had overseen the construction of a new, state-of-the-art shipyard in Quincy. This facility boasted extensive machine shops, foundries, carpentry shops, and vast storehouses, making it one of the largest and most capable shipyards in the United States. The yard had barely opened its gates when the Navy awarded it contracts to build the battleships *Rhode Island* and *New Jersey*, a testament to the company's reputation for high quality and cost-effectiveness.

The same congressional act that authorized the construction of *Nevada* also mandated an eight-hour workday for battleship construction. This progressive labor practice increased costs from $177.25 to $215.26 per ton, as noted in the *Annual Report of the Navy Department for Fiscal Year 1912*. Fore River embraced this change and went beyond the letter of the law, fostering a vibrant workplace culture that included glee clubs, sports teams, and a newsletter highlighting family events. Despite these efforts to create a positive work environment, *Nevada*'s construction would still be marred by twelve separate strikes.

With the contract secured, Fore River's naval architects and engineers plunged into the intricate work of translating plans into reality. As material orders were placed and construction teams assembled, a scale model of *Nevada* was built to aid in the estimating process and to plan the complex sequence of assembly.

The shipwrights employed a process known as "lofting," creating full-sized paper or wooden templates for each component of the ship. These templates would later be used to guide the cutting of steel plates and the placement of openings for hatches, pipes, and wiring. Given *Nevada*'s immense size, this process alone required a veritable army of draftsmen and carpenters.

Adding to the complexity was the need to shape some of the metal plates with compound curves—bending in two dimensions simultaneously. The bow plates, for instance, had to curve outward along the length of the ship and inward toward the keel, a challenging feat of metalworking.

To safeguard the government's interests during *Nevada*'s construction, the Navy assigned naval constructor Thomas G.

Construction of *Nevada* commenced at the Fore River Shipyard, in Massachusetts, on November 4, 1912, with the laying of the keel, which is visible in the foreground of this photo, facing aft, taken on January 1, 1913. Supported by a wooden cradle is the double hull under construction, consisting of curved frames (the "ribs" of the ship's hull) with the outer bottom below the frames and the upper bottom above the frames. The double bottom would contain spaces for fuel oil, fresh water, feed water, and voids. *National Archives*

Largely hidden within a forest of scaffolding is the hull of *Nevada*, viewed from the port side on April 1, 1913. Toward the left is a frame, with lightening holes cut in it; running forward from the frame is the keel. Several longitudinal bulkheads are visible above the frame. *National Archives*

Roberts of the Bureau of Construction and Repair to oversee the project. Roberts found himself in the unenviable position of bearing responsibility for the completion of the largest ship the Navy had ever constructed, yet lacking direct authority over the shipyard's operations.

On November 4, 1912, nearly ten months after Fore River won the contract, the first tangible steps in *Nevada*'s creation took place. In a large, open space gently sloping toward the river, workmen carefully positioned a line of substantial wooden keel blocks. Once these were in place, they constructed a wooden cradle matching the shape of the ship's bottom around the blocks.

With painstaking precision, skilled ironworkers laid two flat steel plates, each approximately 20 feet long and 4 feet wide, on the forwardmost keel blocks. These plates formed the beginning of the ship's "outer bottom." A vertical plate, parallel to the length of the ship, was then positioned on the seam between the bottom plates to create an inverted T. Two more horizontal plates were added on top, forming an I beam. These upper horizontal plates marked the start of the ship's "inner bottom."

This pattern continued along the entire length of the ship, forming *Nevada*'s keel—the nautical equivalent of a backbone. Unlike the pomp and ceremony that often accompanies modern keel-laying events, there was no formal ceremony to mark this milestone in *Nevada*'s birth. The work simply continued, driven by the urgency of national defense needs and the tight contractual timeline.

From the central keel, the shipwrights worked outward to create the rest of the hull. Plates forming the outer hull were laid flat on the wooden cradle, starting from the keel and extending outward. Vertical plates, running perpendicular to the ship's length, were affixed following the curve of the hull. If the keel was the ship's spine, these vertical plates constituted the beginning of her ribs.

The joints between the hull plates were staggered to increase strength, and rivet and bolt patterns were meticulously designed to transmit stress as evenly as possible. Every aspect of the construction incorporated lessons learned through decades of naval shipbuilding experience.

As the hull took shape, workers began to assemble the sides and the transverse bulkheads—the internal walls running from side to side that divided the ship into watertight compartments. Decks and internal spaces were constructed inside the hull, and the stem—the heavy steel casting forming the bow of the ship—was connected.

On September 10, 1913, the first compartment was tested for watertight integrity, a crucial step in ensuring the ship's survivability in combat. The following month, on October 27, the first armor plate was installed, beginning the process of transforming *Nevada* from a simple hull into a fortress of the sea.

As the hull rose from its wooden cradle, workers installed the ship's power plant. Twelve Yarrow Express water-tube boilers, arranged in three watertight compartments with four boilers each, would drive the engines and a pair of 300-kilowatt dynamos supplying electricity to the ship. These boilers were marvels of engineering, producing steam at 295 pounds per square inch by circulating water through an array of 1,092 tubes, each 1.75 inches in diameter. Seven oil burners heated each boiler, igniting a fine mist of preheated heavy oil to extract maximum energy from the fuel.

Steam from the boilers was directed via 9-inch-diameter pipes to four engine rooms, two on each side of the ship. The high-pressure Curtis turbines in the forward engine rooms, designed to spin at a maximum of 222 rpm, featured massive blades measuring 11 feet in diameter. At full power, each could generate 6,625 horsepower.

To maximize fuel efficiency—a critical factor given the Navy's insatiable desire for long-range capability—the steam exiting the main engines was sent to lower-pressure turbines in the aft engine rooms, generating additional power. Reversing turbines were mounted in the same casing as the low-pressure turbines, allowing the ship to change direction without the need for a separate reversing gear.

In July 1914, a major contract modification provided for the installation of two geared cruising turbines in the forward engine rooms. Manufactured by the General Electric Company, these turbines were designed to increase efficiency at nominal cruising speeds. Each cruising turbine could generate 1,750 horsepower while spinning at 3,200 rpm. A specially designed gearbox reduced this by a factor of 23.85 to connect to the propellers. These cruising turbines were intended for use at speeds below 15.5 knots and could be disconnected at higher speeds.

Nevada's propulsion system culminated in two 14-foot-diameter, three-bladed propellers. Each propeller was cast in a single piece of manganese bronze, a testament to the advanced metallurgy of the time. At the ship's normal load, the top of each propeller would be nearly 14 feet below the surface of the water, helping ensure smooth operation even in rough seas.

As *Nevada*'s hull and machinery took shape, work was also progressing on her armament. Tests of a full-scale mockup of the revolutionary triple-gun turret were conducted at the Naval Proving Ground during 1912. The results were deemed "satisfactory," albeit "subject to minor modifications." This news came as a relief

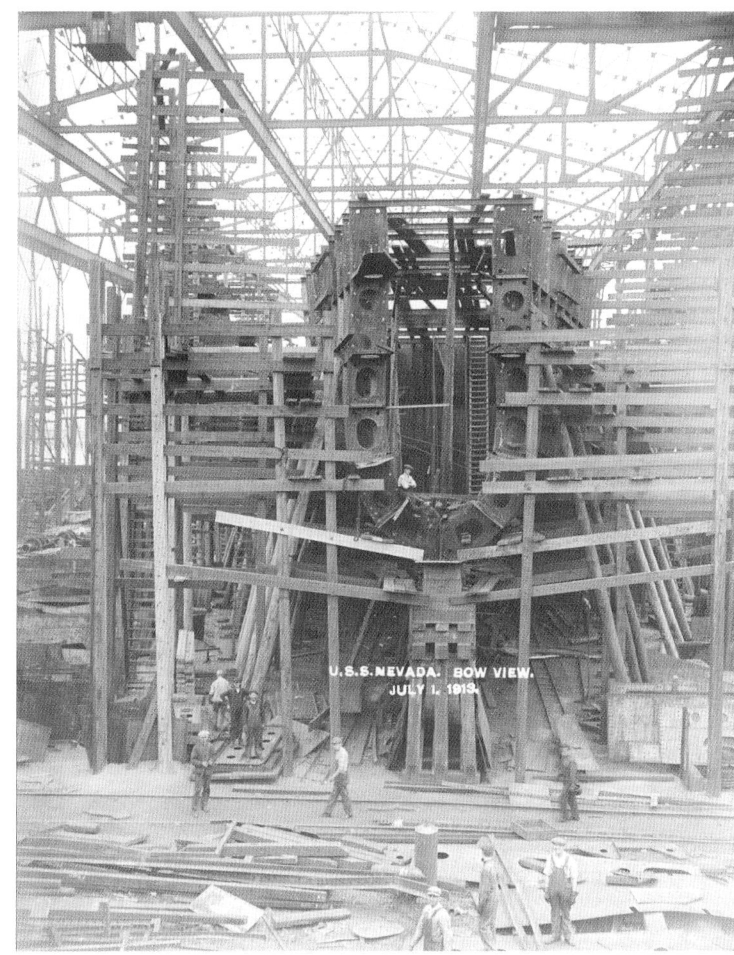

The bow is shown shortly before completion, on July 1, 1913. Below the bow is the forward end of the series of wooden keel blocks that support the structure during construction. *National Archives*

An elevated view of the hull of *Nevada* dated July 1, 1913, faces forward. At the top of the structure are the beams—lateral supports—for the third deck. The outer parts of this deck, which also was referred to as the watertight deck, would slope downward. *National Archives*

Also taken on July 1, 1913, was this photo of the hull of *Nevada*, facing aft, with the curved beams for the third deck visible. Farther aft, steel plates have been riveted to the beams. Later, the armored belt, which would provide protection from torpedoes and shells above and below the waterline, would be installed along the sides of the third deck. *National Archives*

The port bow of *Nevada* is viewed from the port side on October 1, 1913. This battleship would feature a bulbous bow, and the curved framing for that structure is visible toward the left. *National Archives*

In another photograph dated October 1, 1913, the third deck is observed facing aft. In the foreground is a transverse bulkhead at frame number 30 (the ship's frames were numbered consecutively from the bow to the stern). Just aft of the bulkhead is an opening for barbette 1, a heavily armored cylinder that will support turret 1. Aft of that opening is barbette 2. *National Archives*

to both the Bureau of Ordnance and the Bureau of Construction and Repair, since manufacture of the actual turrets was already well underway by the end of that year.

On July 11, 1914, twenty months after the first keel plates were laid, USS *Nevada* was ready for launching. The event drew a distinguished crowd of guests, including Secretary of the Navy Josephus Daniels, Assistant Secretary (and future president) Franklin D. Roosevelt, Nevada governor Tasker Oddie, Massachusetts governor David Walsh, and several members of Congress. VIPs crowded shoulder to shoulder on a reviewing platform facing the massive bow of the ship, while hundreds of spectators lined the ways. Admission to the yard was by ticket only, prompting many to take to the river in small boats or stand on the shore opposite the shipyard for a glimpse of the spectacle.

The honor of christening *Nevada* went to ten-year-old Eleanor Anne Siebert, niece of Governor Oddie. As she swung a 1-quart bottle of Mumm's Extra Dry Champagne, wrapped in red, white, and blue ribbon, against the bow, saying, "I christen thee *Nevada*," workmen cut away the last restraints holding the hull in position. The cradle carrying *Nevada* slowly began to slide backward into the river. Despite the application of 8 tons of grease to ease her progress, the friction caused smoke to flare from the skids.

Once *Nevada* was in motion, the challenge became keeping her from picking up so much speed that she would cross the Fore River and run aground on the other side. To retard her motion, heavy ropes and chains connected the cradle carrying the ship to stakes sunk into the ground. Each of these "stops" snapped in turn, momentarily slowing the ship's progress.

The launch went off without a hitch, and following the formal ceremony, Fore River president J. W. Powell hosted a luncheon for 130 dignitaries at the Copley Plaza Hotel in Boston. Among other gifts, Miss Siebert was presented with a diamond-studded gold locket to commemorate the occasion.

While the launching marked a significant milestone, much work remained before *Nevada*'s raw hull was transformed into a fighting ship. The spectacle of *Nevada*'s launch barely subsided before work resumed in earnest. As dignitaries departed, a fleet of tugs maneuvered the massive hull to a nearby dock. Here, the arduous task of transforming the bare hull into a fully equipped battleship began.

By mid-August 1914, a mere month postlaunch, *Nevada* stood at 72 percent completion. However, the remaining work encompassed some of the most crucial and complex systems. The

In a photo taken on April 1, 1914, construction of barbette 1 continues. Immediately aft of this barbette is barbette 2, with barbette 3 visible in the background. *National Archives*

Faintly visible behind the scaffolding in a photo dated April 1, 1914, is the bulbous bow of *Nevada*, now fully sheathed. The sign on the front of the keel block toward the lower left reads "HULL 205 U.S.S. NEVADA." *National Archives*

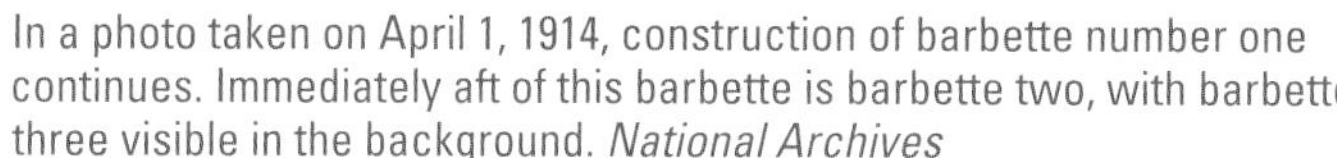

In a photo taken on April 1, 1914, construction of barbette number one continues. Immediately aft of this barbette is barbette two, with barbette three visible in the background. *National Archives*

In the foreground of this April 1, 1914, photograph facing forward above the second deck, to the lower right is barbette 4, with barbette 3 just forward of it. In the distance is barbette 2. *National Archives*

installation of side armor, turrets, guns, and myriad other equipment lay ahead.

Nevada's protective shell took shape as workers affixed the armor belt along her sides. This formidable barrier measured 13.5 inches thick above the waterline, gradually tapering to 8 inches below. The Bureau of Construction and Repair had foresightedly contracted for 15,300 tons of Krupp-type armor, to be shared between *Nevada* and her sister ship *Oklahoma*. This massive order was distributed among three industrial giants: Bethlehem Steel, Carnegie Steel, and Midvale Steel.

The main turrets received particularly impressive protection. Their forward faces boasted a staggering 18 inches of armor plate, while the cylindrical barbettes supporting them and facilitating ammunition transfer were encased in 13-inch-thick armor. This level of protection positioned *Nevada* among the world's best-armored battleships of her time.

Nevada's primary armament, a marvel of engineering in its own right, came to life under the guidance of the Washington Navy Yard. Four separate manufacturers contributed to the production of her 14-inch guns. Each of these behemoths stretched 52.5 feet in length—a staggering forty-five times their diameter—and tipped the scales at over 140,000 pounds. Their construction involved a series of concentric steel tubes, further reinforced by steel hoops. The innermost tube, precision-engineered with spiral rifling grooves, would impart a stabilizing spin to shells as they rocketed down the barrel.

The ship's silhouette was defined by two towering masts, each soaring 114 feet above the waterline. These weren't simple poles, but intricate "cage" designs woven from steel pipes in a spiral pattern. This innovative structure provided robust strength while minimizing the risk of complete collapse from a single enemy hit. Atop these masts, crews would man spotter platforms, operate searchlights, and manage radio antennae, serving as *Nevada*'s eyes and ears in battle.

As *Nevada* inched closer to completion, the world beyond the shipyard descended into chaos. The summer of 1914 saw escalating international tensions erupt into open conflict. The assassination of Archduke Franz Ferdinand in Sarajevo set off a chain reaction of declarations of war, quickly engulfing Europe in what would become known as the Great War. While most Americans hoped to remain aloof from this "European dispute," the conflict lent new urgency to *Nevada*'s completion.

However, the path to *Nevada*'s readiness was not smooth. A series of setbacks—including labor strikes, rejected materials, and tardy deliveries—pushed her projected completion date to mid-August 1915, a delay of nearly eight months from the original schedule.

This delay did not go unnoticed in Washington. In early January 1915, Representative A. P. Gardner of Massachusetts pressed Secretary of the Navy Josephus Daniels for an explanation. Daniels's response painted a picture of compounding challenges: strikes had cost fifty-three days, material rejections another seventy-five, and late deliveries a further seventy-five. Various other issues beyond the shipyard's control had added up to a total delay of ten months.

As *Nevada*'s major systems came online, each underwent rigorous testing. Unanticipated problems often arose, requiring modifications that consumed precious time to design, fabricate, install, and validate. The Navy's patience wore thin with what it perceived as foot-dragging by Fore River Shipbuilding.

This frustration boiled over in late September 1915, when naval constructor T. G. Roberts penned a scathing letter to his superior at the Bureau of Construction and Repair. Roberts accused the contractors of aiming for a timeline "wholly incompatible with state of the work on this vessel." He warned that Fore River appeared intent on postponing "a whole lot of testing until after the trials," a strategy Roberts found deeply concerning.

A pivotal moment arrived on Sunday, October 3, 1915, when steam first coursed through *Nevada*'s portside main and cruising turbines. These engines, representing the cutting edge of marine propulsion technology, required installation tolerances measured in thousandths of an inch. Even the slightest misalignment of the massive 11-foot-diameter rolled-brass turbine blades could lead to catastrophic failure.

Less than a week later, *Nevada*'s starboard engines underwent similar trials, yielding equally positive results. These initial tests employed only low-pressure steam to prevent damage to the dock where *Nevada* was moored. The successful powering of these turbines marked one of the final hurdles that *Nevada* needed to clear before leaving the shipyard.

On the morning of October 22, 1915, *Nevada* finally bid farewell to Fore River Shipbuilding Company. As she steamed past Boston Light at 11:10 a.m., she flew not the Stars and Stripes, but the flag of Fore River Shipbuilding. Though *Nevada* was not yet commissioned into the US Navy, she was about to face her first true test—the open sea.

At the helm stood Capt. Joseph Kemp, Fore River's thirty-two-year-old marine superintendent. With five years of experience guiding new ships from the yard, Kemp knew *Nevada* and the river and possessed the steady nerves required for such a delicate operation.

Nevada's departure was a ballet of precision seamanship. The narrow confines of the Weymouth Fore River, barely 1,000 feet

The bow of *Nevada* was photographed on July 1, 1914, ten days before her launching. Through its streamlined design, a bulbous bow acted to enhance the ship's fuel economy and stability. *National Archives*

The hull of *Nevada* is seen from astern on July 1, 1914. As the day of launching, July 11, approached, the multitude of wooden braces and shores that supported the hull would be methodically removed so as not to interfere with the launching. *National Archives*

At the launching of *Nevada*, Eleanor Anne Siebert, age ten (*center*), a niece of Governor Tasker Oddie of Nevada (*right*), would break the ceremonial bottle of champagne on the bow, part of the christening of the ship. To the left is Secretary of the Navy Josephus Daniels. *Library of Congress*

Eleanor Anne Siebert is poised with the ceremonial bottle of champagne at the christening of *Nevada*. Part of Miss Siebert's duties as the ship's sponsor was to announce the ship's name just before smashing the bottle on the bow. *Library of Congress*

wide at the shipyard with a channel less than 110 feet across, demanded utmost caution. *Nevada*'s massive propellers, if engaged, would only churn up sediment and create unpredictable currents. Instead, a team of tugs, their movements orchestrated by Kemp and his handpicked assistants, gently guided the 575-foot leviathan through the tight passage.

A temporary catwalk spanning *Nevada*'s breadth gave Kemp an unobstructed view as they navigated past the center swing bridge just north of the shipyard. This marked the first time a battleship of *Nevada*'s size had traversed the newly dredged eastern channel, adding an extra layer of tension to the maneuver. With painstaking care, it took a full twenty minutes to ease *Nevada* through the gap.

Once clear of Quincy Bay's constraints, Capt. Kemp called for steam to *Nevada*'s turbines. For the first time, the ship moved under her own power, her massive engines propelling her into the Atlantic. Kemp maintained a cautious approach during this maiden voyage. While *Nevada*'s systems had been tested dockside, they had never before faced the dynamic stresses of open-ocean travel.

As *Nevada* passed Boston Light, she encountered her first ocean swells. Every rivet, weld, and joint were now subjected to a thousand new stresses, a trial by sea that would truly test the quality of her construction. The Navy's insistence on strict quality control during the building process was about to be put to the ultimate test.

While most individual components had been thoroughly examined before *Nevada* left the yard, this voyage would reveal how well they functioned as an integrated whole. Kemp anticipated some teething problems, and his expectations were met. On the first night out, a pump in the steering compartment short-circuited. The following morning, rudder control had to be shifted from the steam-driven unit to the electrical backup. A test of the cruising engine was cut short when a thrust bearing on the starboard turbine overheated. These were minor issues, easily addressed once they reached New York, but they highlighted the complexity of bringing such a massive and intricate machine to life.

Nevada was not due in drydock until October 25, giving Kemp three days to put her through her paces. As he grew more confident in her seaworthiness, he gradually increased power to the main turbines. At 215 rpm, just shy of their 222 rpm design maximum, *Nevada* surged forward at 19 knots. Kemp felt certain that once *Nevada*'s hull was cleaned and smoothed in drydock, she would easily achieve her design speed of 20.5 knots, possibly even pushing 22 knots at full power.

This strong performance from *Nevada*'s engines came as a relief to Kemp. The memory of turbine problems in the earlier

Fore River Shipyard workers and spectators watch as *Nevada* slides down the ways during her launching, on July 11, 1914. Draped on the forecastle is the American flag. *Library of Congress*

After *Nevada* slid off the ways and came to a stop in the Fore River, tugboats came alongside to maneuver her to a fitting-out dock, where construction of the ship would continue. *Library of Congress*

Fore River–built *North Dakota* was still fresh, and debate continued in naval circles about the suitability of turbine propulsion for capital ships. A second problematic vessel would have been a severe blow to Fore River's reputation.

At 2234 on October 24, *Nevada* dropped anchor off Tompkinsville, Staten Island. There was no need to risk a nighttime passage into drydock, and both the Navy and Fore River were eager to maximize the publicity value of *Nevada*'s arrival in New York.

The following morning, *Nevada* began her stately progress up New York Harbor, escorted by a flotilla of tugs and pleasure craft packed with onlookers eager to catch a glimpse of the Navy's newest battleship. By late morning, she was safely ensconced in Dry Dock 4 at the New York Navy Yard, ready for the final preparations that would transform her from an impressive hull into a fully operational warship, prepared to defend the nation in an increasingly turbulent world.

In the months leading up to *Nevada*'s arrival, the *New York Times* had been whipping up public anticipation. The newspaper lauded the ship as a revolutionary vessel, declaring, "In appearance, in arrangement of her batteries, and in many other important ways the *Nevada* is a ship the like of which was never before seen in New York." This media attention transformed *Nevada*'s debut into a much-anticipated event, a symbol of national pride and technological achievement.

As *Nevada* made her way to Dry Dock 4, she was greeted by throngs of spectators eager to catch a glimpse of this marvel of naval engineering. However, for naval constructor T. G. Roberts, there was no time for celebration. The day after *Nevada* left Fore River, Roberts dispatched a scathing thirty-page letter to the secretary of the Navy, detailing his frustrations with the shipbuilder's approach to completing the vessel.

Roberts's missive included an exhaustive list of 597 items that he deemed necessary for completion before considering the ship ready for service. These ranged from minor issues such as repairing gaskets and stopping small leaks to more-significant tasks such as fitting locking devices on watertight hatches and patching seams in ducts. It was, in essence, a punch list akin to what a home buyer might provide to a builder before taking possession.

Roberts was adamant that Fore River should address these items before *Nevada* underwent her formal trials. His concerns had already reached Washington; even as his letter was en route, he received a directive from David W. Taylor, chief of the Bureau of Construction and Repair. Taylor instructed Roberts to immediately telegraph Washington if the outstanding items were not progressing satisfactorily or if they remained incomplete when *Nevada* departed New York.

On October 28, at 1330, *Nevada* left Dry Dock 4. She made her way back to Tompkinsville before embarking on a leisurely journey to Rockland, Maine, the site chosen for her formal trials. Traveling at low speed, *Nevada* didn't reach Rockland Breakwater until 0705 on October 30.

With the formal inspection not scheduled to begin until November 3, Capt. Kemp seized the opportunity to conduct his own series of tests on *Nevada*. Lt. Mathewson reported: "At 6:45 a.m. 31 October 1915, the ship got underway and made runs at various speeds over measured mile for Contractors' benefit at speed varying from 10 knots to full power. The average of the three longest full power runs was 20.707 knots per hour." *Nevada* had bested the contractually required maximum speed by just over 0.2 knots.

Tugboats assist *Nevada* to the fitting-out dock. Temporarily fastened along much of the side of the hull is wooden planking where the belt armor will later be installed. Flying above barbette 3 is the Fore River Shipyard corporate flag. *National Archives*

Almost three months after her launching, *Nevada* is being fitted out at Fore River Shipyard, on October 1, 1914. Alongside the hull is a barge with a crane, which is lifting a heavy object, causing the barge to list to port. *National Archives*

***Nevada* General Data, 1916**	
Dimensions	
Length overall	583'0"
Waterline length	575'0"
Maximum beam	95'2½"
Deep draft	29'7"
Builder	Fore River Shipbuilding Company, Quincy, Massachusetts
Laid down	November 4, 1912
Launched	July 11, 1914
Commissioned	March 11, 1916
Displacement	
Standard	27,500 tons
Full load	28,400 tons
Armor Protection	
Total armor weight	7,835.3 tons.
Belt	13.5 inches tapering to 8", 17'4 5⁄8" wide, 8'6" below water
Armor deck	50 lb. STS + 50 lb. STS + 20 lb.; aft 180 lb. STS + 70 lb. amidships
Splinter deck	40 lb. NS + 20 lb. / 60 lb. NS + 20 lb. STS + 20 lb./60 lb. STS + 20 lb.
Turrets, faceplates	18"; sides: 16"/5" STS / 10"–9"
Barbettes	13"
Conning tower	16" + 50 lb. STS / 5" STS
Armament	
Main battery	10 14"/45
Secondary battery	21 5"/51
Torpedo tubes	2 21" (submerged)
Machinery	
Total weight	1,900 tons (with liquids)
Boilers	12 Yarrow 295 psi
Engines	Curtis turbines
Shaft horsepower	26,500 maximum ahead
Maximum speed	20.5 knots
Endurance	12 knots: 5,195 nautical miles
Rudders	1, balanced.
Fuel	2,042.8 tons oil
Complement	864 total (55 officers, 809 enlisted)

Workers labor aboard *Nevada* at the fitting-out dock at Fore River Shipyard on October 1, 1914. Rising above and to the immediate rear of barbette 2 is the conning tower; above the tower is a crane mounted on a barge on the starboard side of the ship. Belt armor has been installed along the port side of the hull from the aft part of the hull to approximately abeam barbette 1. Forward of that point, the wooden planking is still on the side of the hull. *National Archives*

In a photo dated January 4, 1915, the large crane on the fitting-out dock is lowering a 14-inch/45-caliber gun onto turret 1. On the dock floor below the crane are two gunhouse assemblies, consisting of the rears and sides of the units. The large, tubular object on the dock to the front of the crane is one of the king posts for the two boat cranes. *National Archives*

In a view of *Nevada* from above her port quarter deck on January 1, 1915, in the foreground is turret 3 before the gunhouse was installed, with the cradles for the two 14-inch/45-caliber guns in view. The round structure on the deck immediately forward of that turret marks where the cage mainmast will be installed later. Farther forward is the upper deck, which extends to the forecastle. On that deck, the raised cylinder with the white canvas cover over it is the base of the smokestack, also referred to as the smoke pipe. *National Archives*

The gunhouse of turret 1 had been installed by the time this photograph was taken on January 4, 1915. Turret 1 was armed with three guns, while turret 2 had two guns. Scaffolding and staging planks are on the side of the hull, and installation of the belt armor is complete. *National Archives*

In a photo taken on April 6, 1915, the cage foremast is under construction, and the smokestack has been substantially completed. The king post for the port boat crane has been erected just forward of turret 3. The 5-inch/51-caliber guns have been mounted on the superstructure deck and in the casemates along the upper hull. The frontal shield and the front part of the roof of turret 1 have not yet been installed. *National Archives*

Nevada is viewed off her port bow on July 6, 1915. Constructed of spirals of curved steel tubes in a form in geometry known as a hyperboloid of revolution, cage masts were lightweight, strong, and durable and able to withstand multiple direct hits. *National Archives*

Turret 3 is in the foreground of this photo of *Nevada*, facing forward, on July 6, 1915. The roof of turret 4 is at the bottom, below turret 3's 14-inch guns. Forward of turret 3 are nine large cowl vents, for funneling fresh air belowdecks. The scoops could be rotated in a direction to most efficiently catch a breeze. To the sides of the vents are the two boat cranes. *National Archives*

The status of work on *Nevada* as of July 7, 1915, is documented in this view of the battleship from the starboard side. Hanging on the side of the hull are numerous scaffolding frames, from which most of the planks have been removed. The main-battery director station still remains to be installed atop the foremast, and the main mast has not been erected yet. *National Archives*

Nevada was nearing completion when this photo was taken at Fore River Shipyard on October 1, 1915. The mainmast had been installed and main-battery director tubs and searchlight platforms had been mounted on both masts. A temporary wing bridge had been built to the sides of the conning tower, for the use of observers during the tricky navigation out of the shipyard. *National Archives*

On October 22, 1915, *Nevada* steamed out of the Fore River Shipyard and into the Atlantic, proceeding to drydock at the New York Navy Yard, where her lower hull would be scraped and repainted and her propellers polished. *Library of Congress*

After leaving drydock in New York, *Nevada* proceeded to waters off Rockland, Maine, where she was subjected to manufacturer's sea trials, to identify and correct any mechanical deficiencies. Here, *Nevada* is proceeding at 16.13 knots during a speed trial on November 3, 1915. The trials would determine whether the ship could attain its required maximum speed of 20.5 knots. *National Archives*

Nevada had achieved a speed of 19.51 knots, just 1 knot below its mandated maximum speed, when this photo was taken on November 3, 1915. The bow wave is about to cause trouble for a small craft to the far right, which had approached too close to the battleship. *National Archives*

The ship was making 16.11 knots at the moment this photo was snapped on November 3, 1915. On the stern is a casemate-mounted 5-inch/51-caliber gun. US Navy experience would show that casemate guns were problematic because of their proximity to the waterline and their susceptibility to saltwater spray. *National Archives*

Nevada is steaming at 17.5 knots in this photo taken during speed trials on November 3, 1915. The ship was able to achieve an average maximum speed of 20.707 knots over its three-longest full-speed tests: a fraction of a knot more than its mandated maximum speed. *National Archivesv*

An undated view of *Nevada* on a hazy day in an unidentified port contains a clue about its likely date, although it is visible only under high magnification. Up and down each side of the stem (the front of the bow) are painted, in white, a scale of horizontal lines with numbers. These markings appear exclusively in photos of the manufacturer's sea trials between November 1915 and January 1916. *Library of Congress*

A final photo of *Nevada*'s speed trials on November 3, 1915, shows the battleship steaming at 17.5 knots. The temporary port wing bridge is visible aft of turret 2. The thick black smoke seen in these speed-trials photos was a result of a faulty mixture of fuel and air in the boilers. *National Archives*

After the builder's trials, *Nevada* steamed back to the Fore River Shipyard for further work. She is seen here, high in the water, at Fore River on January 10, 1916. The shutters for the casemate embrasures, which were lowered when the 5-inch guns were readied for action, are closed, with the gun barrels protruding through embrasures in the covers. *National Archives*

CHAPTER 2

Commissioning and Shakedown

Capt. William Sowden Sims's selection as *Nevada*'s first commanding officer befitted the ship's status as the world's most powerful battleship. A Naval Academy graduate, Sims had earned a reputation as a reformer and rebel within the Navy. His dedication to improving naval efficiency, particularly in gunnery, had caught President Theodore Roosevelt's attention, leading to his appointment as naval aide.

Sims arrived at Fore River in October 1915, eager to shape the newest battleship into the fleet's finest vessel. On November 1, 1915, Board of Inspection members began their review, joined by VIPs including David W. Taylor, chief of the Bureau of Construction and Repair, and RAdm. Victor Blue, chief of the Bureau of Navigation.

Formal trials ran from November 3 to 10, 1915. *Nevada* passed every test, but several items still required attention before commissioning. As weeks passed, Washington pressed for swift delivery, concerned about the war in Europe. By late February, the Navy Department wanted the ship in Boston by March 1.

On March 10, 1916, T. G. Roberts reported from Boston that Fore River had nearly completed all work. The acting commanding officer, Cmdr. J. T. Tompkins, pushed for commissioning on March 11, driven by the cost of keeping supplies on the dock and the desire to avoid the inauspicious thirteenth. The Navy Department agreed, authorizing immediate delivery with only five items of work unfinished.

Capt. Sims was absent during these proceedings, testifying before the House of Representatives Committee on Naval Affairs in Washington. On March 10, he spent the day answering questions on various naval matters, unable to attend to his ship's commissioning, but that was not to be all—the committee informed him he was expected to continue testifying on the upcoming Tuesday, which meant he would miss the commissioning of his ship.

Nevada's commissioning took place on March 11, 1916, at the Navy Yard in Boston. Her log entry recording:

> FROM 1:42 to 2:00 PM
>
> At 1:42 with the USS NEVADA moored to the south west side of pier #9, Navy Yard, Boston, Mass., with the officers and crew in mass formation on the after end of the main deck, and after Commander R. D. Hasbrouck, US Navy, captain of the yard, read telegraphic orders from the Navy Department authorizing the acceptance of the ship from the Fore River Ship Building Corporation, in accordance with contract agreement and directing that ship be placed in commission, the national colors and commission pennant were hoisted in accordance with the ceremonies prescribed by the Navy Regulations.

Cmdr. J. T. Tompkins assumed command in Sims's absence, addressing the crew: "This is a great day for the Navy. The *Nevada* is without doubt the finest ship in this part of the world and one of the most powerful of any navy in the world." Chief Boatswain C. W. Antonson led three cheers for the ship.

Capt. Sims reported aboard on March 16, 1916. Three days later, *Nevada* opened to the public, with over two thousand visitors marveling at the technological wonder. On March 23, *Nevada* left Boston, arriving at the New York Navy Yard two days later for further outfitting.

After more than two months in New York, including time in drydock, *Nevada* departed for Newport, Rhode Island, on May 25 for mini-shakedown cruises. The ship then proceeded to Hampton Roads, Virginia, for gun trials. On May 22, 1916, gun crews tested the 5-inch secondary armament, followed by the 14-inch main battery the next day.

Nevada's ten 14-inch guns could fire 1,400-pound armor-piercing shells up to 23,000 yards accurately. Each gun used four silk bags containing 365 pounds of smokeless powder. The first shot resulted in an accident, with Chief Turret Officer C. N. Curtis suffering injuries from a recoiling gun.

The following day, *Nevada* demonstrated her full potential with a ten-gun salvo. Nearly 2 tons of explosive propelled the shells, creating a deafening noise and erupting flames from the ship's sides. For several minutes after the salvo, *Nevada* gently rocked side to side.

Capt. Sims quickly established his unique leadership style aboard *Nevada*. He believed in fostering initiative by delegating work and spent hours communicating with crew members. The crew soon became accustomed to their captain suddenly appearing before them with the admonition "Cheer up!" The phrase was the title of Sims's favorite poem, written in December 1914 by James R. Gooding, which read as follows:

Nevada was commissioned at Pier 9 at Boston Navy Yard on March 11, 1916. The original complement of the ship, called the commissioning crew, is assembled on the fantail as the commissioning ceremony unfolds. The commissioning marked the formal transfer of the ship from the builder to the US Navy, and it was at that time that "USS" (United States Ship) was added before the ship's name. *Naval History and Heritage Command*

We cannot, of course, all be handsome,
And it's hard for us all to be good—
We are sure now and then to be lonely,
And we don't always do as we should.

To be patient is not always easy,
To be cheerful is much harder still—
But at least we can always be pleasant
If we make up our mind that we will.

And it pays every time to be kindly,
Although you feel worried and blue—
If you smile at the world and be cheerful,
The world will smile back at you.

So try to brace up and look pleasant,
No matter how low you are down—
Good humor is always contagious,
But you banish your friends when you frown.

The phrase "Cheer up!" quickly became *Nevada*'s unofficial motto, earning her the nickname the "Cheer-Up Ship."

Sims had the poem printed on cards and posted throughout the ship. Crew members created a mat for his stateroom with the motto and installed an electric "Cheer Up!" sign behind his desk. Sims's spirit proved infectious, and word that *Nevada* was a good ship spread quickly through the fleet.

Sims emphasized collective ownership, encouraging use of "we" and "our." He understood that many crew members were young and away from home for the first time. During one extended stay in Boston, *Nevada*'s crew reported no incidents of drunkenness or desertion, remarkable for the era. This dedication translated into excellent performance ratings.

William Sims maintained his tradition of afternoon tea aboard *Nevada*, insisting on high standards. Initially, the tea service was a makeshift affair, much to Capt. Sims's chagrin, inspiring him to write to the paymaster general of the Navy, saying, "Our junior officers are serving tea in a pitcher or a three-inch cartridge case, cream in a toothbrush mug. This is not proper for a first-class battleship. Assuming, therefore, that you are an advocate of adequate preparedness, can you allow us enough for tea tools? Peary drank tea at every meal on the dash for the Pole and I take it every afternoon. It is the warrior's beverage." Later in 1916, the state of Nevada presented its namesake battleship with a magnificent sixty-eight-piece silver service made from 300 pounds of Nevada silver and gold, certainly exceeding Sims's expectation of tea tools.

After a brief Philadelphia stop, *Nevada* joined the Atlantic Fleet. On July 10, 1916, she took position astern of *Arkansas* for tactical and battle maneuvers, including a realistic war game. *Nevada* was finally fulfilling her designed purpose, steaming with the Atlantic Fleet to protect American shores.

August 1916 saw *Nevada* again with the fleet. On August 8, she narrowly avoided colliding with *Arkansas*. On August 11, the ships practiced attack formations, taking turns playing enemy roles and learning valuable lessons about engagement strategies and responses to surprises. On September 27, while anchored in New York, *Nevada* listed to starboard by about 3 degrees. Soundings revealed the ship was aground on the port side, but she refloated with the rising tide without damage.

William Sims received promotion to rear admiral in August 1916, a long-overdue recognition of his contributions. While the promotion allowed him to choose his next assignment (he opted for president of the Naval War College), it meant never again commanding a ship. Sims left *Nevada* on December 30, 1916, amid thunderous cheers from the crew.

Capt. Joseph Strauss, former head of the Bureau of Ordnance, replaced Sims. Strauss had spent much of his career developing the weapons that Sims had perfected in practice, including the 12-inch gun of early US dreadnoughts. Like Sims, Strauss had a practical bent, establishing the Naval Proving Ground at Indian Head, Maryland.

After a New Year's Day in Norfolk, Strauss took *Nevada* to sea on January 9, 1917. A week's battle practice preceded "cruising in the Caribbean Sea," with stops in Puerto Rico, Haiti, and Cuba. On January 24, torpedo defense exercises saw destroyer flotilla ships "attack" the battleship line, reaching *Utah* immediately astern of *Nevada* but never achieving a firing position on the "Cheer-Up Ship."

Life aboard a warship in the tropics was challenging. Men sweated, and food spoiled quickly. A ton and a half of potatoes had to be jettisoned due to rot. Boiler room crews appreciated *Nevada*'s oil-fired system, sparing them from shoveling coal in extreme heat.

The commissioning crew of *Nevada* is lining the rails off Boston Navy Yard sometime in March 1916. Ship's boats are stored aft of the smokestack and on the davits alongside the afterdeck. *Randy Fagan, The Floating Drydock collection*

Nevada presents her starboard side off Boston on March 23, 1916. Immediately aft of turret 2 is the conning tower, the heavily armored control center of the ship. Between the top level of the conning tower and the foremast is the chart house, above which is the navigating bridge, an open-topped structure with a canvas canopy rigged over it. On the rear of the roof of turret 3 is a platform, for future installation of two antiaircraft guns. *Library of Congress*

On the same date the preceding photo was taken, *Nevada* is viewed from the forward-starboard quarter off Boston Navy Yard. Several crewmen are standing on the starboard wing bridge. *National Archives*

Also taken on March 23, 1916, was this view of *Nevada,* proceeding at low speed in Boston Harbor. The battleship was beginning a cruise to the New York Navy Yard for further work, including the mounting of torpedo tubes and ammunition hoists. *National Archives*

USS *Nevada* is proceeding out of Boston Harbor, en route to the New York Navy Yard, on March 23, 1916. Two searchlights with white covers over the lenses are on a platform on the lower part of the mainmast. *National Archives*

USS *Nevada* is underway at sea in or around March 1916. The shadow on the side of the hull outboard of turret 4 and just above the waterline marks the beveled aft edge of the belt armor. At the upper right is the aft torpedo defense platform, and toward the left is the port boat crane. *Library of Congress*

Nevada spent much of February at Guantánamo Bay, the fleet's winter headquarters. The bay accommodated the entire Atlantic Fleet while leaving room for seaplane operations. Recreational facilities ashore included swimming pools, tennis courts, baseball diamonds, and a golf course.

During this period, the fleet practiced torpedo defense, gunnery, and various maneuvers. On February 28, VAdm. DeWitt C. Coffman, commander of the Battleship Force, observed target practice aboard *Nevada*. The ship fired ten rounds from her main guns at targets 20,000 yards away, continuing after lunch with single-gun shots and two-gun salvos.

March 6 proved challenging when the electric steering gear failed three times. After the third failure, Strauss switched to the steam-driven steering system for the rest of the day. Despite these setbacks, *Nevada* completed her assigned gunnery drills.

Torpedo practice on March 8 became an exercise in trust. *Nevada* fired two torpedoes at a target towed by *Wyoming*, achieving "partial hits." When *Wyoming* fired at a target towed by *Nevada*, one torpedo struck *Nevada* herself. Fortunately, because it was a practice torpedo, it caused no damage.

The fleet returned to Norfolk, remaining there until the end of March. Sports competitions occupied the ships' crews, with *Nevada* winning first place in punt and dinghy boat races.

A final photo from March 23, 1916, shows *Nevada* steaming out of Boston Harbor. The ship's name is faintly visible in raised letters on the hull, slightly forward of the stern casemate gun. *National Archives*

At the end of 1916, USS *Nevada* spent time in Dry Dock 4 at the US Navy Yard, Norfolk, Virginia, as seen in a photo taken on December 29. In the spirit of the season, a Christmas tree is propped up on the roof of turret 1. The ship was equipped with two anchors on the port side, as seen here, and one on the starboard side.

CHAPTER 3

World War I and Interwar Years

When the United States declared war against Germany on April 6, 1917, *Nevada* was undergoing repairs at the Norfolk Navy Yard in Portsmouth, Virginia. After refueling on April 20, she required additional repairs following equipment tests. *Nevada* finally got underway on April 24, anchoring with the fleet in Hampton Roads, Virginia.

Initially part of Battleship Division 8 (BatDiv8), later a unit in the Battleship Force, *Nevada* trained gunners in the Chesapeake Bay, operating from Norfolk. On August 13, she cleared Cape Henry with the Battleship Force, bound for Long Island Sound. The force anchored off Base 10 at Port Jefferson, New York, on August 19, conducting tactical and gunnery training until October 1. Returning to Hampton Roads on October 6, *Nevada* disembarked two Russian navy officers who had been aboard since September 30.

On October 25, after several days of rehearsals, *Nevada* conducted short-range battle practice and returned to Lynnhaven Roads, Virginia. Through November and December 1917, based at Norfolk, she continued to train her crew in preparation for combat deployment. On December 7, 1917, Adm. William S. Benson, Chief of Naval Operations, ordered the removal of two 5-inch guns, mounts, accessories, and spare parts from *Nevada* and several other battleships.

As 1918 began, *Nevada* continued tactical maneuvers and gunnery training. On July 30, 1918, Adm. Benson informed VAdm. Sims of plans to counter potential German battle cruiser raids against supply lines and troop convoys. Battleship Division 6 (BatDiv6), including *Utah*, *Nevada*, and *Oklahoma*, was to be stationed at Queenstown or Brest. Battleship Division 5 (BatDiv5), comprising *Arizona*, *Mississippi*, *New Mexico*, and *Pennsylvania*, would cover the western Atlantic or proceed as necessary.

On August 12, 1918, *Nevada* and *Oklahoma*, under RAdm. Thomas S. Rodgers, sailed from Hampton Roads, arriving at Bantry Bay, Ireland, on August 23. Stationed at Berehaven and designated the Bantry Bay Squadron, this force aimed to counter potential German high-speed raiders in the Atlantic. *Utah* joined on September 10. *Nevada* missed planned gunnery practices and tactical drills later that month when accompanying minesweepers were withdrawn prematurely.

On October 10, 1918, the Admiralty and Navy Department agreed to protect troop convoys following reports of German battle cruisers in the Atlantic. RAdm. Rodgers ordered his division, screened by seven destroyers, to rendezvous with two inbound convoys. The battleships escorted the convoys through the danger zone before detaching. Despite the reports, German ships never sortied, and the transports were never in danger from surface raiders.

Spanish influenza struck Berehaven in late October 1918. During the week of October 26, seven of *Nevada*'s crew died, along with four each from *Oklahoma* and *Utah*. A hospital was established, and strict quarantine was enforced. By November 10, few influenza cases remained in the force, though two additional *Nevada* sailors died that week. During the outbreak, drills were limited to fire control and fire distribution exercises conducted at anchor.

The armistice ending hostilities took effect on November 11, 1918. On November 18, *Nevada* steamed for Rosyth, Scotland, escorted by destroyers *Stockton*, *McCall*, *Davis*, and *Trippe*, to join Battleship Division 9 (BatDiv9), operating with the British Grand Fleet as Battle Squadron 6. She arrived too late to witness the German High Seas Fleet's surrender on November 21.

Nevada then shifted to Portsmouth, England, rejoining BatDiv6. On December 11, 1918, VAdm. William S. Sims, commander of US naval forces in European waters, arrived and assumed command. The ships prepared to escort President Woodrow Wilson to Brest, France. On December 13, they rendezvoused with the transport *George Washington*, carrying President Wilson, and the US Atlantic Fleet flagship *Pennsylvania*. Each ship rendered a twenty-one-gun salute as the transport passed. On December 14, the battleships departed Brest for the United States.

Encountering heavy seas en route, the battleships entered New York Harbor on December 26. They passed the yacht *Mayflower*, with Secretary of the Navy Josephus Daniels aboard, anchored off the Statue of Liberty. Each ship fired a nineteen-gun salute before anchoring in the North River. Battalions from various ships paraded through New York, celebrating the war's end.

In 1919, amid rising US-Japan tensions, President Wilson transferred several warships to the Pacific. *Nevada* transited the Panama Canal, arriving at San Pedro, California, on August 9. She then cruised with other US ships, visiting ports along the Pacific coast.

Nevada later returned to the East Coast, rejoining the Atlantic Fleet in Battleship Division 7 (BatDiv7). On July 17, 1920, she was redesignated BB-36. With *Arizona* (BB-39) as flagship, *Nevada*, *Oklahoma*, *Pennsylvania*, *Utah*, *Delaware* (BB-28), and *North*

Around 1917, USS *Nevada* (*left*) is moored alongside the battleship USS *Florida* (BB-30) at the St. Helena training station, Norfolk, Virginia. By the time this photo was taken, a wedge-shaped fairing had been installed on the front of the navigating bridge, and a more substantial frame had been furnished for the canopy over the navigating bridge: These features are evident in some of the subsequent photos.

Dakota (BB-29), BatDiv7 arrived at Guantánamo Bay, Cuba, for winter training on January 9, 1921.

The division then moved to Colon, Canal Zone, and after transiting the Panama Canal rendezvoused with the Pacific Fleet under Adm. Hugh Rodman for night battle practice off Panama. The combined fleets headed south, crossing the Equator, and the Atlantic Fleet ships visited Callao, Peru, arriving on January 31. After a week's stay, they rejoined the Pacific Fleet for athletic competitions in Panama. *Nevada*'s race-cutter team defeated *Arizona*'s for the prestigious Battenberg Cup.

During summer 1921, *Arizona*, *Nevada*, and *Oklahoma* returned to Callao (July 22–August 3) for the Peruvian Centennial Exposition. *Nevada* then departed for the US, stopping at Balboa, San Diego, and San Francisco before reaching San Pedro on September 8. She remained there until November 18, when she visited San Francisco, returning to San Pedro on December 3.

On January 19, 1922, *Nevada* sailed to San Francisco, staying until February 15. Returning to San Pedro on February 17, she remained until May 6, when she departed for the East Coast. En route to Norfolk, she visited San Diego and Balboa, arriving at Norfolk Navy Yard on May 31. After maintenance and time in Hampton Roads, *Nevada* and *Maryland* (BB-46) embarked on a goodwill tour for Brazil's independence centennial on August 18. They visited Rio de Janeiro and Santos before returning to Hampton Roads on December 9.

While *Nevada* was en route to the US on December 6, a general order reorganized the Navy, creating the United States Fleet. The Battle Fleet, based in the Pacific, included most battleships, while the Scouting Fleet, in the Atlantic, comprised older battleships and other units. The Atlantic-based Control Force protected trade routes and defended against amphibious attacks. The Asiatic Fleet, Naval Forces Europe, Special Service Squadron, and submarine force remained independent.

Nevada departed Norfolk on January 13, 1923, returning to the Pacific. After gunnery exercises and tactical training at Guantánamo (January 17–February 12), she shifted to Culebra Island en route to the Canal Zone. Transiting the Panama Canal on February 23, she arrived at San Pedro on April 11. *Nevada* spent much of the latter half of 1923 visiting Washington cities and underwent maintenance at Puget Sound Navy Yard from October 9 to December 1.

On January 2, 1924, *Nevada* departed for the Caribbean and Atlantic. She conducted various exercises and port visits, including New York, before returning to San Pedro on April 22. After

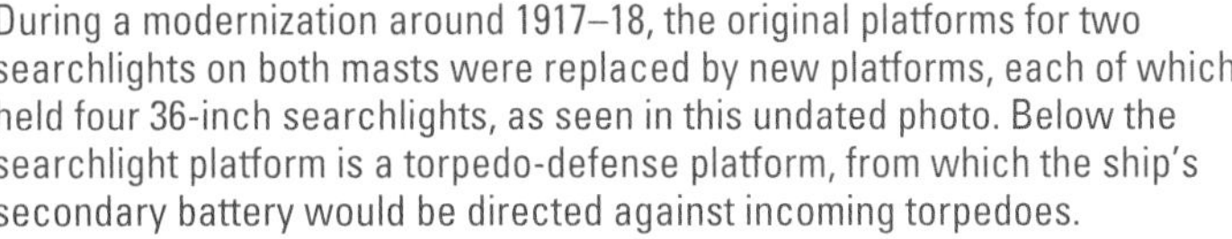

During a modernization around 1917–18, the original platforms for two searchlights on both masts were replaced by new platforms, each of which held four 36-inch searchlights, as seen in this undated photo. Below the searchlight platform is a torpedo-defense platform, from which the ship's secondary battery would be directed against incoming torpedoes.

One of *Nevada*'s cage masts, likely the mainmast on the basis of the number of reinforcing rings above the searchlight platforms, is viewed in an undated photo. The two searchlight platforms (*bottom*) originally were separate structures until they were replaced by single platforms holding four searchlights in the 1917–18 period. At the top is the spotters' top, a tub in which spotters directed the fire of the ship's main battery.

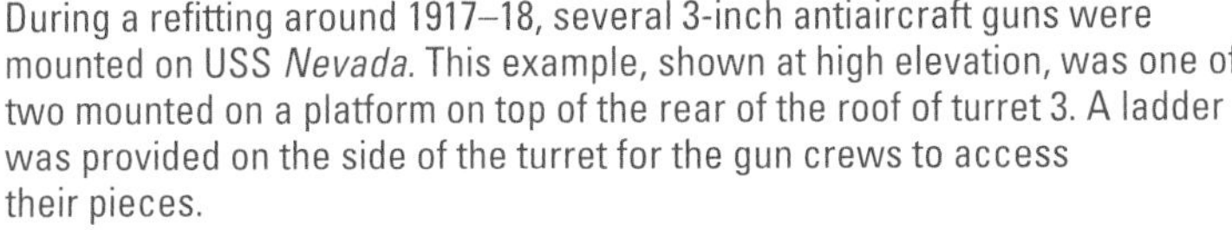

During a refitting around 1917–18, several 3-inch antiaircraft guns were mounted on USS *Nevada*. This example, shown at high elevation, was one of two mounted on a platform on top of the rear of the roof of turret 3. A ladder was provided on the side of the turret for the gun crews to access their pieces.

In the days before shipboard observation aircraft, US battleships employed lighter-than-air observation balloons to allow observers to scan for distant threats and to spot artillery fire, to enhance the accuracy of the ship's main battery. Here, *Nevada*'s observation balloon is being inflated on the fantail.

Nevada was photographed from her observation balloon, most likely in 1917. The wing bridges are still present, and the "cloverleaf" platforms for four searchlights, features dating from late 1916, are discernible on the cage masts. The deflection scales that would be painted on turrets 2 and 3 by the time the ship departed for Europe in 1918 are not yet present. *Naval History and Heritage Command*

For a limited time around 1917–18, USS *Nevada* was painted in a splinter camouflage scheme, as shown here in a photo that was assigned the date of May 11, 1918. This disruptive camouflage was designed to confuse enemy fire-control spotters as to the relative bearing and speed of the battleship. *National Archives*

maintenance at Puget Sound Navy Yard from late June to August, she made port visits along the West Coast before returning to San Pedro on September 8. *Nevada* entered Puget Sound Navy Yard again on December 8 for an overhaul lasting until February 2, 1925.

Returning to San Pedro on February 8, 1925, *Nevada* conducted training and port visits in California. On April 15, she departed San Francisco with the fleet for war games in Hawaiian waters, concluding on May 29. The fleet then prepared for a goodwill tour that came to be known as "the Great Cruise" to Australia and New Zealand. *Nevada*, with ten battleships, four light cruisers, thirty-two destroyers, and thirteen auxiliaries, left Honolulu on July 1.

The fleet conducted tactical maneuvers en route, refueling at Pago Pago, Samoa (July 9–11), before reaching Melbourne on July 22. After a successful stay in Australia, *Nevada* sailed for New Zealand on August 6, arriving at Wellington on August 11. The fleet departed for the US on August 24, stopping at Samoa and Pearl Harbor. After meeting Assistant Secretary of the Navy T. Douglas Robinson on *Arizona*, the Battle Fleet passed in review and anchored at San Pedro on September 26.

Nevada began 1926 with a stay at Puget Sound Navy Yard from January 6 to February 19. She then visited various ports, including Balboa and Port Culebra, Costa Rica, before returning to San Pedro on April 1. Corroded condensers temporarily prevented *Nevada* from operating with the Battle Fleet, earning her the nickname "Pond Lily." However, her rowing team won the fleet cutter races, reclaiming the Battenberg Cup.

In early 1927, *Nevada* underwent repairs at Hunter's Point, San Francisco, before departing for the Caribbean. She visited Balboa, Cristobal, Gonaïves, and Guantánamo, conducting training exercises. After repairs at Norfolk Navy Yard, she visited the US Naval Academy at Annapolis and made port calls along the East Coast.

Nevada then returned to the West Coast, arriving in San Diego on June 27, 1927. After brief stops in San Francisco and San Pedro, she headed back to the East Coast, transiting the Panama Canal on August 2. She shuttled between Guantánamo and Gonaïves before proceeding to Annapolis, arriving on August 25. Following a port visit to Baltimore, *Nevada* returned to Norfolk Navy Yard on September 14. On September 16, 1927, she was placed in reduced commission for modernization.

Nevada was late in joining the US Fleet in Europe after the US entry into World War I, being the last US battleship to arrive in European waters, in late August 1918. USS *Nevada*, USS *Utah*, and USS *Oklahoma* combined to form Battle Ship Division 6 (BatDiv 6), based at Bantry Bay, Ireland, for the duration of the war. Here, *Nevada* leads a column of warships around late 1918. The recently modernized navigating bridge, with fixed windows and roof, is discernible. A close inspection of the photo reveals that a deflection scale (also called azimuth scale) had been painted on the side of turret 2. This scale, which was black with a white scale and numbers, will appear more clearly in subsequent photos. It allowed nearby friendly battleships to train their guns on the same bearing, in order to achieve concentration of fire. Also, recently installed on the front of the foremast just above the searchlight platform concentration dial, or range clock, a large, white disk with two movable "clock" hands, by which the ship's fire control team could signal other battleships the range at which the 14-inch guns were firing. *Naval History and Heritage Command*

Weapons and Ballistics							
Weapon	**Ammo type**	**Gun model**	**Projectile mark**	**Projectile weight**	**Explosive charge**	**Muzzle velocity**	**Range yards**
14"/45 cal.	armor piercing	8	3	1,400 lbs.	31.5 lbs	2,600 fps	21,000
14"/45 cal.	armor piercing	8	20	1,500 lbs.	22.9 lbs	2,600 fps	23,000
14"/45 cal.	high capacity	8	19	1,275 lbs.	104.2 lbs.	2,735 fps	23,500
5"/51 cal.	common	13	15	50 lbs.	4.3 lbs.	3,150 fps	17,100
5"/51 cal.	high capacity	13	39	50 lbs.	26.4 lbs.	3,150 fps	17,100
3"/50 cal.	APCBC	21	29	13.1 lbs.	1.2 lbs.	2,700 fps	29,800
3"/50 cal.	high capacity	21	27	13.1 lbs.	5.7 lbs.	2,700 fps	29,800
3"/50 cal.	AAC	21	27	13.1 lbs	5.7 lbs.	2,700 fps	29,800

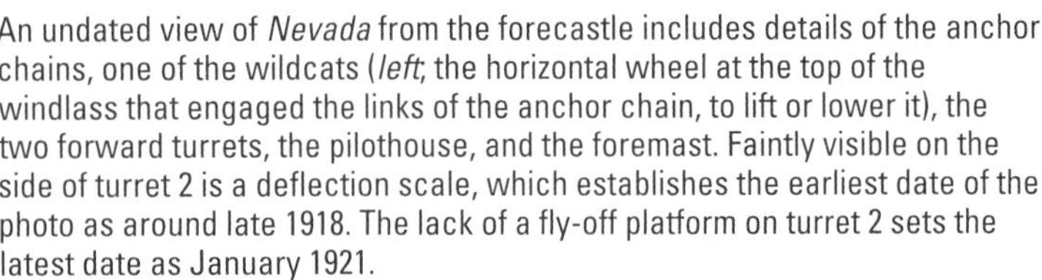

An undated view of *Nevada* from the forecastle includes details of the anchor chains, one of the wildcats (*left*; the horizontal wheel at the top of the windlass that engaged the links of the anchor chain, to lift or lower it), the two forward turrets, the pilothouse, and the foremast. Faintly visible on the side of turret 2 is a deflection scale, which establishes the earliest date of the photo as around late 1918. The lack of a fly-off platform on turret 2 sets the latest date as January 1921.

USS *Nevada* was photographed from the air off Brest, France, while serving in a convoy that escorted President Woodrow Wilson to Brest in December 1918. The recently rebuilt navigating bridge, octagonal in plan, has a rangefinder on its roof. On the hull abeam the navigating bridge, boat booms have been extended, for mooring boats to. Much of the ship's crew has assembled on the weather decks, clad in dress blues and white caps. *Naval History and Heritage Command*

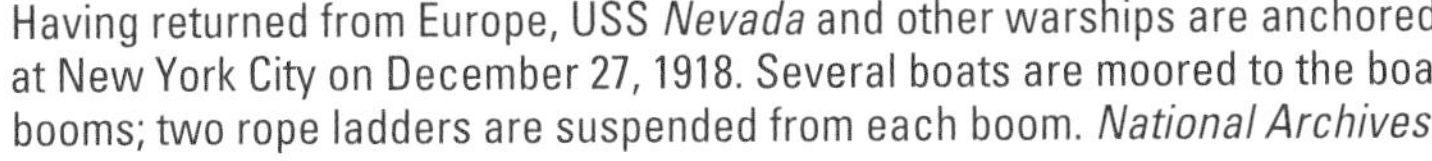

Having returned from Europe, USS *Nevada* and other warships are anchored at New York City on December 27, 1918. Several boats are moored to the boat booms; two rope ladders are suspended from each boom. *National Archives*

This photo was taken moments from the preceding one, showing more of the port side of the ship. On the preceding day, December 26, *Nevada* and other ships of the fleet sailed in review in New York Harbor. *Naval History and Heritage Command*

USS *Nevada* is observed from the aft-starboard quarter at New York on December 27, 1918. At the same time the forward range clock and deflection scale were added to the ship, an aft range clock was installed on the rear of the mainmast, and a range scale was painted on the gunhouse of turret 3. The 5-inch gun had been removed from the stern casemate. *Naval History and Heritage Command*

In early 1919, USS *Nevada* steamed to Guantánamo Bay, Cuba, to participate in fleet maneuvers. In this photo taken around early March of that year, the battleship is anchored at Guantánamo with an observation balloon moored to her fantail. The balloon was tethered to the ship during its time aloft, and an observer occupied a backet suspended below the balloon. *Naval History and Heritage Command*

A photographer in a floatplane snapped this shot of USS *Nevada* anchored off New York City on April 23, 1919. Life rafts are stored on the roofs of turrets 1 and 4 and on the sides of the barbettes of the other two turrets. *Naval History and Heritage Command*

The first USS *Wisconsin* (BB-9), *right*, and USS *Nevada*, *left*, are in, respectively, Dry Docks 4 and 3 at the Norfolk Navy Yard on May 19, 1919. An Illinois-class pre-dreadnought battleship launched in 1898, *Wisconsin* would be decommissioned almost exactly a year later.

The port side of *Nevada*'s quarter deck is viewed facing forward around 1919. The two boats are marked "NEV 5" and "NEV 2" on their transoms. At the lower right is a horizontal deck capstan. *Naval History and Heritage Command*

By the time this photo of *Nevada* was taken at the Norfolk Navy Yard, on June 4, 1920, fly-off platforms had been constructed on the roofs of turrets 2 and 3 to allow observation aircraft to launch from the ship. For launching the aircraft, the ship would sail directly into the wind, allowing the planes to take off from the very short platforms. *Naval History and Heritage Command*

Awnings are rigged over the forecastle, alongside turret 2, and over the fantail of *Nevada*, anchored at Guantánamo Bay, Cuba, in January 1920. The shutters of the casemates have been opened to air out the compartments. On each side of the hull, the 5-inch guns had been removed from one forward and three aft casemates on each side of the hull, as well as the stern casemate, and the openings were permanently covered with steel panels with portholes. *National Archives*

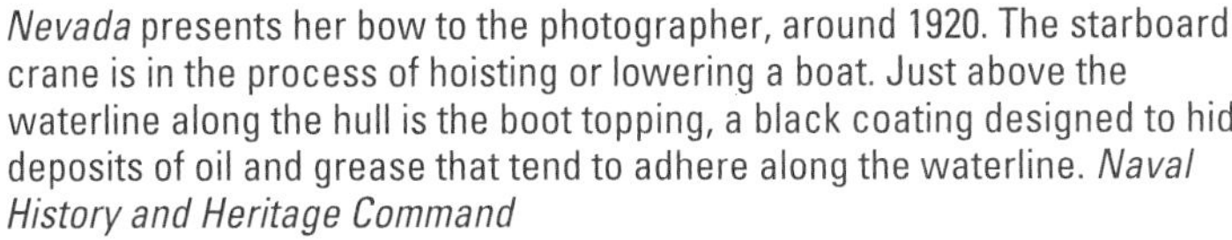

Nevada presents her bow to the photographer, around 1920. The starboard crane is in the process of hoisting or lowering a boat. Just above the waterline along the hull is the boot topping, a black coating designed to hide deposits of oil and grease that tend to adhere along the waterline. *Naval History and Heritage Command*

The forward turrets, the pilothouse, and the foremast of *Nevada* are shown in this backlit photograph at Guantánamo Bay around January 1920. A close inspection of the photo reveals that subcaliber guns are clamped to the center barrel of turret 1 and the left barrel of turret 2, just in front of the frontal armor of the gunhouses. Subcaliber guns were small guns that were fired during training exercises, to save on the cost of firing real 14-inch shells. *Naval History and Heritage Command*

USS *Nevada* is observed broadside in Guantánamo Bay around January 1920. Rangefinders are present above the pilothouse and on the rear of turret 3's roof. *Naval History and Heritage Command*

The port side of *Nevada* is depicted at Guantánamo Bay around January 1920. The plated-over embrasures of the forward and aft casemates are visible below the muzzles of the 14-inch guns of turret 1 and above the boat moored toward the stern. The 5-inch gun of the stern casemate also had been permanently removed. *Naval History and Heritage Command*

Signal flags are flying from the yardarms of the mainmast of *Nevada* at Guantánamo in January 1920, and bedding has been strung over the rails along the decks to air out. *Naval History and Heritage Command*

Capt. William D. MacDougall, commanding officer of USS *Nevada*, is being piped over the side of the battleship in Guantánamo Bay in January 1920. Capt. MacDougall was commanding officer of *Nevada* from October 23, 1919, to May 4, 1920. Standing guard to the left are members of the Marine detachment of *Nevada*. *Naval History and Heritage Command*

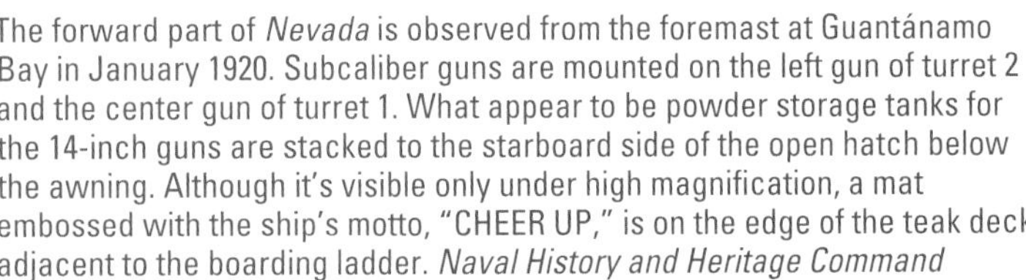

The forward part of *Nevada* is observed from the foremast at Guantánamo Bay in January 1920. Subcaliber guns are mounted on the left gun of turret 2 and the center gun of turret 1. What appear to be powder storage tanks for the 14-inch guns are stacked to the starboard side of the open hatch below the awning. Although it's visible only under high magnification, a mat embossed with the ship's motto, "CHEER UP," is on the edge of the teak deck adjacent to the boarding ladder. *Naval History and Heritage Command*

The mainmast and the afterdeck are observed from the foretop at Guantánamo Bay around January 1920. Four 36-inch searchlights are mounted on the platform on the mainmast. Below that platform is the aft torpedo-defense platform, from which spotters would direct the fire of the ship's secondary battery against incoming torpedoes. *Naval History and Heritage Command*

While in Guantánamo Bay on January 14, 1920, a minor fire broke out on the ship. Crewmen are standing by turret 2 while smoke issues from the superstructure. *National Archives*

In another photo taken during the fire of January 14, 1920, to the left, next to the barbette of turret 2, is a paravane, a towed, winged, underwater device designed to destroy submerged mines. At the center is a 5-inch/51-caliber gun. *National Archives*

Nevada is anchored in the Hudson River off Riverside Drive, Manhattan, on May 3, 1920. Two different observation planes are on the fly-off platforms: a Sopwith 1½ Strutter with a large number 5 on the fuselage on the forward platform, and a Nieuport 28 on the aft one. *Naval History and Heritage Command*

In an aerial photo dating to June 1920, the Sopwith 1½ Strutter numbered 5 is on the forward fly-off platform. On the superstructure deck adjacent to the conning tower are a 5-inch gun and, to its rear, a 3-inch antiaircraft gun.

Nevada is viewed from above on September 10, 1920. Bedding is draped over the rails, to air out. Both masts were painted black above the level of the top of the smokestack, to mask the soot that accumulated from the smoke.
National Archives

As seen from the front of the foremast, a Sopwith 1½ Strutter is spotted on the fly-off platform atop turret 2, around 1921. On the horizontal stabilizers are elevator locks, each of which had two wooden slats that went over and under the stabilizers to immobilize the elevators, to prevent damage to them from high winds. *Naval History and Heritage Command*

Nevada rides at anchor in an undated photograph. It was taken some time between the first appearance of fly-off platforms on the ship around January 1920 and the replacement of those platforms by catapults before February 1923. *National Archives*

In January 1921, *Nevada* steamed to the Pacific via the Panama Canal, to participate in joint maneuvers by the Atlantic and the Pacific Fleets. After a visit to Callao, Peru, *Nevada* and the Atlantic Fleet proceeded north to rendezvous with the Pacific Fleet. During that transit, a photographer in the foretop took this rare close-up photo of the maintop. Two crewmen are visible in the main-battery station. The platform had a conical roof and a curved wind deflector around the upper part of the tub. Aft of *Nevada* is a battle line, with main batteries trained to the port side. *Naval History and Heritage Command*

Accompanied by a tugboat, USS *Nevada* navigates the Culebra Cut of the Panama Canal. Though this photograph is undated, the image was published in the Washington, DC, *Star* on March 6, 1921, and the original probably was taken during *Nevada*'s transit of the Panama Canal in mid-February 1921.

USS *Nevada* is lying off Coco Solo, near the Caribbean-side entrance to the Panama Canal, in August 1921. The previous month, the Navy announced that several of its newer battleships, including *Nevada*, were going to be transferred soon to the Pacific Fleet. *National Archives*

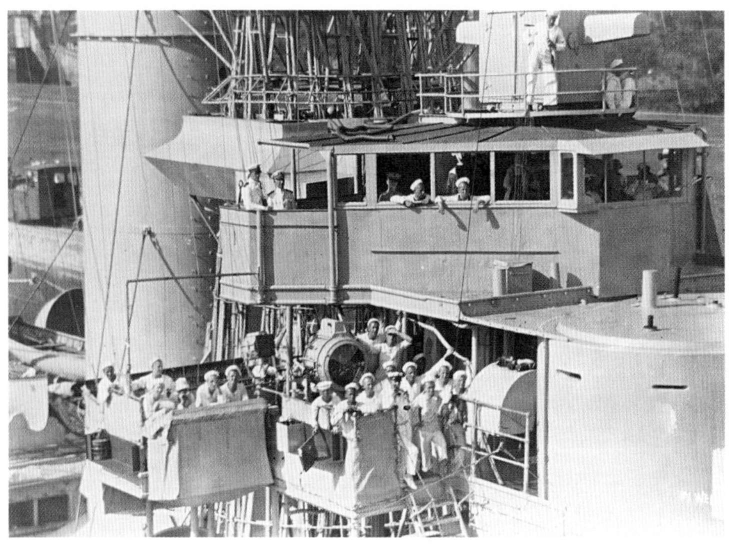

This remarkable photo of the navigating bridge of *Nevada* was taken during one of the ship's transits of the Panama Canal, around 1921. On the roof is a rangefinder, to the rear is the foremast, and to the lower right is the top of the conning tower, with several vision slits in view. At the lower left is the starboard flag board, where signal flags were stored; inboard of the flag board are two searchlights. *Naval History and Heritage Command*

Crewmen of USS *Nevada* pose for their photograph in a saloon, possibly in the Caribbean or South America around 1921. Two of the sailors have brought a guitar and a banjo, to provide entertainment for their crewmates. *Naval History and Heritage Command*

Ships of the Pacific Fleet would conduct oar-powered boat races, to foster a competitive spirit and boost morale. This whaleboat crew from USS *Nevada* became the champions of the Pacific Fleet by taking first place in the boat races at San Pedro Bay, California, on October 15, 1921. *Nevada*'s commanding officer, Capt. Douglas E. Dismukes, is standing at the center. *Naval History and Heritage Command*

The crew of one of *Nevada*'s 5-inch/51-caliber casemate guns is performing a drill around 1921. The second crewman from the right is barefoot; although it would seem to defy the laws of safety, USN ships' crewmen often are seen barefoot in vintage photos as they went about their duties. To the rear of that man, another is holding the breechblock-operating lever of the gun. *Naval History and Heritage Command*

Around 1921, USS *Nevada* (*foreground*) is steaming in formation with other ships, including her sister ship, USS *Oklahoma* (BB-37). Fly-off platforms and deflection scales are present on turrets 2 and 3. *Naval History and Heritage Command*

This series of three photographs showing bountiful details of *Nevada* from the starboard side is undated but was taken some time between around January 1921, when the fly-off platforms were installed on turrets 2 and 3, and around February 1923, when the platforms were removed. Seen here are turrets 1 and 2, trained to starboard; the boarding ladder; the conning tower with its vision slits; the superstructure and enclosed pilothouse; and the foremast. The boat to the left is marked "NEV 3" on the bow.

The casemate-gun shutters often were opened when the ship was in port. They were hinged on the bottom and consisted of eight panels that could be locked together or unlocked to allow for opening individual panels. Each shutter had three portholes and an oblong opening for the 5-inch gun barrel. Above the casemate openings are what appear to be rolled-up curtains. Two levels above the casemates, on the superstructure deck, are a 3-inch antiaircraft gun and a 5-inch/51-caliber gun.

A boat is moored to the boat boom on the starboard side of *Nevada* aft of turret 3. On the edge of the deck above the boom is the king post, to which was rigged a cable for supporting the boom. Suspended from the boom is a rope ladder. The two slightly recessed rectangular areas with four portholes each, on the hull, were formerly gun casemates that were deleted and plated over in 1919.

USS *Nevada* is at Newport News, Virginia, in early January 1923, following a goodwill tour to Brazil. Recently installed on the fantail were an aircraft crane and a catapult, mounted on a turntable in order to turn the aircraft into the wind for launching. On the catapult is what appears to be a Vought VE-7 observation plane. No longer needed, the fly-off platforms had been removed from turrets 2 and 3.

Nevada is at anchor at an unidentified location on February 28, 1923, a few days after participating in a fleet problem off the west coast of Panama. Spotted on the fantail next to the catapult is a biplane floatplane. A new 3-inch antiaircraft gun mount had been installed on a round platform on each side of the mainmast. *National Archives*

Puget Sound Navy Yard, in Bremerton, Washington, in November 1923. A sailor sitting on a plank is touching up the "NEVADA" name near the stern. Blast bags are fitted over the 14-inch barrels of turret 4 where the barrels enter the frontal armor, but turret 3 lacks the blast bags. Also called bucklers, these fixtures sealed out the elements from the interiors of the gunhouses. *Puget Sound Naval Shipyard*

During a visit to Bremerton on July 29, 1923, members of the orchestra of *Nevada* pose for their photograph. On the bass drum and on the banjo, "CHEER UP ORCHESTRA" reflects *Nevada*'s "cheer up" motto. *Naval History and Heritage Command*

This elevated view of *Nevada* taken from above her stern was marked with the year "24" (1924). It was published by the firm of Sponagel & Herrmann, who were based in San Francisco; presumably, that was where the photo was taken. A biplane is spotted on the catapult. *USS Tennessee Museum*

Turrets 1, 2, and 4 as well as the starboard 5-inch/51-caliber of USS *Nevada* are trained to starboard on March 27, 1925, during Grand Joint Army-Navy Exercise Three, off Oahu, Territory of Hawaii. On that date, *Nevada* conducted a shore bombardment in advance of an amphibious-landing exercise. *National Archives*

Nevada was photographed in Hawaiian waters on May 6, 1925, from an altitude of 1,000 feet. White awnings are rigged next to the superstructure deck and around the mainmast. Two observation planes are spotted on the catapult, and a third one is on the starboard side of the fantail.

Nevada is at anchor at Pearl Harbor on May 29, 1925. An observation plane is discernible on the catapult. The cargo ship USS *Antares* (AG-10) is in the left background. *National Archives*

Nevada is moored along 1010 Dock at Pearl Harbor on June 6, 1925. A crewman standing atop the pilothouse is signaling, using semaphore flags. The vertical chains on the sides of the bow were part of the paravane system. Stretching down to the forefoot at the bottom of the bow, the chains formed a continuous loop to which the forward end of the tow cable of the paravane was fastened. Hauling on the chains acted to draw the front of the tow cable far below the waterline, for proper operation of the paravane. *National Archives*

The cage masts and the fighting tops, as the main-battery director stations were sometimes referred to, are observed from above the port side of *Nevada* at Pearl Harbor on June 27, 1925. As seen from above, the yardarms had a wishbone shape, with the space between the forks rigged with safety nets. *National Archives*

In the summer of 1925, USS *Nevada* and other ships of the US Fleet participated in the Great Cruise, a goodwill visit to Australia. Here, *Nevada* (*lower left*) and three other ships are moored to Prince's Pier in Melbourne. To the lower right is USS *Pennsylvania* (BB-38), while in the background are USS *Oklahoma* (BB-37) and the armored cruiser USS *Seattle* (ACR-11).

The four US warships are viewed from a different perspective at Prince's Pier, with *Nevada* the closest. All three battleships have observation planes on their catapults. Between the time that *Nevada* was photographed in early July and her appearance in Melbourne in July, the deflection scales on turrets 2 and 3 had been painted over.

The four warships are viewed from above the landside of Prince's Pier, Melbourne, with *Nevada* alongside the end of the right side of the pier. The deflection scales remained on the sides of USS *Pennsylvania*'s turrets 2 and 3.

This aerial photo of the four US warships at Prince's Pier was not taken on the same occasion as the preceding photos. Here, awnings have been rigged over most of the afterdeck of *Oklahoma*, and the awning has been removed from the afterdeck of *Seattle*.

After returning from the Great Cruise, *Nevada* is navigating a narrow channel in Pearl Harbor, on September 17, 1925. An "E" award for excellence is now present on the smokestack. Depending on the color, the "E" signified excellence in gunnery (white), engineering (red), or aviation (green). *National Archives*

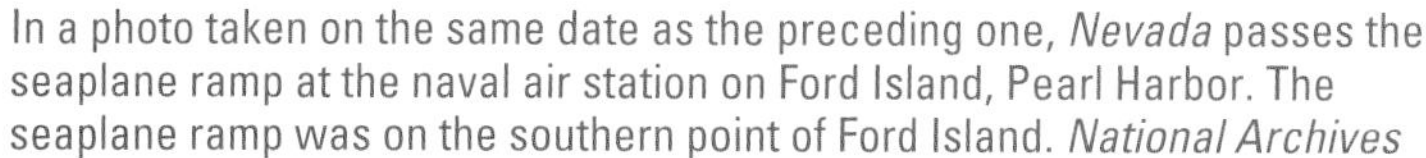

In a photo taken on the same date as the preceding one, *Nevada* passes the seaplane ramp at the naval air station on Ford Island, Pearl Harbor. The seaplane ramp was on the southern point of Ford Island. *National Archives*

On August 27, 1925, USS *Nevada* is exiting the narrow channel from Pearl Harbor. White canvas awnings are rigged alongside the superstructure. An observation plane is faintly visible on the catapult. *National Archives*

This photo of USS *Nevada* at sea and the following photo were dated June 4, 1927. At this time, *Nevada* was hosting the annual Midshipmen's Cruise of the US Naval Academy, during which cadets learned the craft of manning and operating a battleship firsthand. Two observation planes are spotted in tandem on the catapult. *National Archives*

USS *Nevada* is viewed from her aft-starboard quarter during the Midshipmen's Cruise. The observation planes probably are Vought UO-1s, two of which are known to have been serving with *Nevada* in July 1927. *National Archives*

Four members of the US Navy's brass are posing with Mayor James Rolph of San Francisco, California (*second from right*) in front of City Hall, San Francisco. The occasion was very likely an official visit during the Midshipmen's Cruise in the summer of 1927. To the left is Clarence Selby Kempff, commanding officer of USS *Nevada* from June 1926 to September 1927. Next are T. A. Kearney, commanding officer of USS *Oklahoma*; George W. Laws, commander of the Practice Squadron (i.e., the ships of the Midshipmen's Cruise); Mayor Rolph; and District Commander Thomas Washington. *Naval History and Heritage Command*

Officers and crewmen watch while one of USS *Nevada*'s observation planes, Vought UO-1 Bureau Number (BuNo) A6613, is launched. The two-seater UO-1 was first flown in late 1922 and entered service with the US Navy the following year. *San Diego Air and Space Museum*

Another of *Nevada*'s UO-1s, side number 6-2, is approaching the shoreline near San Diego, California, on July 8, 1927. *National Archives*

In another photo dated July 8, 1927, the BuNo of UO-1 side number 6-2 is seen, under high magnification, on the vertical fin: A6991. *National Archives*

CHAPTER 4

Modernization and Rebirth

By 1927, much of *Nevada*'s machinery had reached the end of its serviceable life. The first eight months of the year saw a staggering number of equipment failures, highlighting the urgent need for comprehensive overhaul. The ship's portside main engine condenser failed at least eleven times, while the starboard condenser failed no fewer than eight times. On three separate occasions, both condensers failed on the same day, though fortunately not simultaneously. These condensers played a crucial role in the ship's steam cycle, cooling steam from the turbines so it could be reinjected into the boilers. When the condensers failed, the boilers couldn't receive sufficient fresh water, severely impacting the ship's operations.

Boiler failures were almost as frequent, with nine occurring during the same period. Boiler number 6 proved particularly troublesome, accounting for six of these failures. The situation reached a critical point on April 24, 1927, when both steam and electric steering systems failed, forcing *Nevada* to drop out of formation. In a scene reminiscent of old sailing ships, sailors in the steering compartment had to man four 6-foot-diameter wooden wheels to steer the massive battleship by hand.

Exacerbating these mechanical issues were severe personnel shortages, particularly in the engineering department. *Nevada* carried only 50 percent of her approved complement of engineering petty officers, a dangerous deficiency given the increasingly unreliable nature of her machinery. The lack of experienced leadership led to an increase in crew errors resulting from inadequate training, further compounding the ship's operational challenges.

It was clear that *Nevada* required more than routine maintenance; she needed a complete makeover. The United States, constrained by the Washington Naval Treaty's ten-year holiday on capital ship construction, couldn't build new battleships until the early 1930s. Therefore, the only way to address the creeping obsolescence of the fleet was to rebuild the ships already in service.

The Washington Naval Treaty was quite specific about the modifications permitted for existing battleships. No changes were allowed to the size of the main guns, and armor could be altered only to improve protection against evolving air or submarine threats. Furthermore, the total alterations to any given ship could add no more than 3,000 tons to her original displacement.

In modernizing *Nevada* and her sister ship, *Oklahoma*, the Navy aimed to provide them with an offensive punch and armor protection similar to the later Colorado-class battleships, as much as possible within treaty constraints. A key aspect of this upgrade was increasing the range of the Nevada class's main battery. While the 14-inch guns themselves were capable of lobbing shells beyond 30,000 yards, the openings in the front plates of the turrets prevented them from being elevated higher than 15 degrees, limiting their effective range to only 23,000 yards.

The solution seemed straightforward: enlarge the openings to permit a maximum elevation of 30 degrees, allowing the full capability of the guns to be utilized. Congress initially approved funds for these modifications but later reversed its decision under pressure from Secretary of State Charles Evans Hughes. The British Admiralty, still smarting from the terms of the Washington Naval Treaty, argued that changing the maximum gun elevation was illegal. Hughes, eager to maintain good relations with London, accepted this argument.

US Navy lawyers strongly disagreed with this interpretation and, through persistent efforts, eventually convinced Congress to fund the modification. A total of $13,150,000 was allocated for the upgrade of *Nevada* and *Oklahoma*, a substantial investment in modernizing these vital fleet assets.

Despite congressional approval, the ships had to wait their turn for modernization. The Navy's shipyards were already busy converting six old coal-burning battleships to oil fuel while completing construction of the new aircraft carriers *Lexington* and *Saratoga*. *Nevada* arrived in Norfolk on September 14, 1927, but her actual modernization didn't begin until January 2 of the following year.

As *Nevada* prepared for her extensive refit, hundreds of men were transferred to other ships, leaving only a skeleton crew on board. After years of gunnery practice, fleet maneuvers, passages through the Panama Canal, and the Great Cruise, the remaining officers and men found it frustrating to sit motionless in the harbor. Maintaining discipline during periods of inactivity proved challenging, since sailors often found innovative ways to get into trouble.

Adding to the difficulties, *Nevada* was without a commanding officer for six months. Capt. C. S. Kempff left the ship in June 1927, and his replacement, Capt. H. H. Royall, didn't arrive until January 1928. Fortunately, *Nevada* had an ally in Capt. David Todd, the commandant of the Norfolk Navy Yard, who had commanded her during the Great Cruise. Todd's affection for

In January 1928, USS *Nevada* began an extensive modernization at Norfolk Navy Yard. The work was wide ranging, including enlarging the gunports of the turrets to achieve higher elevations (and thus longer ranges), replacing the cage masts with tripod masts, replacing the worn-out turbines and boilers, and a host of other modifications. *Nevada* is shown with her new tripod masts and navigating bridge at Pier Four, Norfolk Navy Yard, on September 4, 1929, midway through the modernization. *National Archives*

his old ship and his adeptness at finding ways to accelerate her rebuild proved invaluable during this transitional period.

As naval architects began planning *Nevada*'s modernization, they found that one improvement often led to another. Substantial upgrades to the fire control systems were necessary to take advantage of the longer range of the main guns. However, the relatively lightweight cage-style masts weren't strong enough to support the new equipment and its associated armor protection.

The masts needed replacement regardless of fire control improvements. During *Nevada*'s voyage to Australia in 1925, the commandant of the Pearl Harbor Navy Yard had reported corrosion in many of the steel tubes forming her masts. A similar warning appeared in a January 26, 1926, report from the Board of Inspection and Survey, noting, "Mast has excessive motion when ship rolling or guns firing. The Board recommends that main mast be entirely rebuilt or removed from the ship." The tubular cage masts creaked and swayed dangerously in heavy seas, and the shock wave from a salvo of the 14-inch guns turned them into giant tuning forks.

The solution was a pair of heavy tripod masts firmly attached to the hull. These could easily support the weight of the new three-story fire control stations and would be much less prone to corrosion than the old cage design. This change would significantly improve the ship's ability to direct its fire accurately at long ranges.

While the Washington Naval Treaty prohibited upgrades to armor except to improve protection against torpedoes and air-delivered bombs, designers found ways to enhance *Nevada*'s defenses within these constraints. To counter torpedo threats, they added a "blister" to the sides of the ship—a thin steel shell mounted 3 feet out from the main hull at the second deck. As the hull turned inward, the separation increased to a maximum of 6.5 feet. This standoff would dissipate the explosive force of a torpedo, while the thinness of the blister would minimize the generation of destructive steel splinters during a blast. New bulkheads were also added inside the hull for additional protection.

The addition of the blister, while undoubtedly improving *Nevada*'s survivability, did raise some concerns. The commander of the Scouting Fleet worried that increasing *Nevada*'s beam to nearly 108 feet might cause difficulties when passing through the Panama Canal, a crucial capability for maintaining a two-ocean navy. There were also concerns about potential damage to the relatively thin plating of the blister when the ship rubbed against docks or canal locks, or when tugs pushed against it.

Nevada is observed from farther away in another photograph dated September 4, 1929. Each of the new fighting tops on the masts incorporated, from the top level down, a main-battery director station, a main-battery control and spotting station, and a secondary-battery control station. The range clocks now were higher on the masts, immediately below the secondary-battery control stations. *National Archives*

Engineer Edward L. Cochrane of the Bureau of Construction and Repair acknowledged that "some inconvenience may develop in Canal transits" but insisted that the ship would still fit. He argued that the protection value of the blister more than compensated for any problems that might be encountered during relatively infrequent Panama Canal passages. In practice, the increased beam did create challenges in the canal, requiring *Nevada* to use considerable power to overcome water resistance in the locks.

While *Nevada*'s side armor was considered adequate protection against anticipated enemy shellfire, her deck armor required strengthening to defend against air attack and improve resistance to shells arriving at steep angles during long-range gun duels with other battleships. To save money, Commandant Todd suggested using special-treatment steel (STS) left over from ships abandoned per the Washington Naval Treaty. The yard had nearly enough plates of the proper thickness and could confirm their quality by checking serial numbers against Navy records. The bureau agreed with this cost-saving measure but insisted on impeccable pedigrees for every plate, given the critical role of this armor in protecting the crew during battle.

Virtually everything in *Nevada*'s machinery spaces warranted replacement. Her turbine engines, in particular, were simply worn out. The chiefs of the Bureaus of Engineering and Construction and Repair devised a clever solution that met the need while staying within budget: They would take the newer turbines from the former battleship *North Dakota*, which were in excellent condition, and install them in *Nevada*.

North Dakota (BB-29) had been disarmed in 1923 under the terms of the Washington Treaty, with plans to convert her into a radio-controlled target ship. Although when commissioned in 1908, *North Dakota* had Curtis direct-drive turbines, these had proven problematic. In February 1915, the engines were damaged while returning from Cuba. A major overhaul in June 1915 aimed to repair or replace the engines to the satisfaction of engineer officers, who found these turbines unreliable. By 1917, more-powerful and more-efficient geared turbines had been installed in *North Dakota*, providing 31,300 shaft horsepower—some 6,000 horsepower greater than her original engines and 20 percent more than *Nevada*'s original power plant.

The Navy decided to transplant *North Dakota*'s decade-old, geared turbines into *Nevada* for only $168,865, compared to an estimated overhaul cost of $220,000 for *Nevada*'s existing turbines, and far less than the cost of new-build engines. The additional horsepower would enable *Nevada* to reach speeds close to her former maximum despite the additional drag induced by the new antitorpedo blister.

Nevada's boilers were also in dire need of replacement. When inspectors from the Board of Inspection and Survey examined them in January 1926, they found numerous plugged tubes. The ship's engineering log noted eighteen tube failures during the previous six months, each taking a boiler out of commission until emergency repairs could be made. The board's report recommended replacing the old boilers rather than undertaking "extensive repairs which could not be otherwise than unsatisfactory with an increasing number of tube failures."

However, not all the problems with the boilers were due to age. Maintenance by the crew was so poor that the board recommended convening a formal court of inquiry to investigate "culpable inefficiency" among engineering officers and men. The senior engineering officer had only six months' experience before coming to *Nevada* and lacked sufficient knowledge to maintain the equipment properly.

While the need for a new power plant was undisputed, work couldn't begin until Congress released the necessary funds. Commandant Todd devised a clever work-around to this delay. He argued that because the reboilering of *Nevada* was necessary regardless of other modernization work, it should proceed in advance of congressional appropriation. Todd further suggested that structural material for these changes should be provided in advance of modernization fund authorization.

Taking initiative, Todd co-opted the ship's crew to start tearing out the old equipment, augmenting them with yard workers who were idle after the early completion of *New York*'s modernization. This proactive approach helped jump-start the modernization process, even as they awaited official funding.

Boiler technology had advanced substantially since *Nevada*'s design was finalized in 1911. Engineers calculated that the twelve Yarrow Express boilers installed at Fore River could be replaced by six modern small-tube units. As an added benefit, the lower fuel consumption of the new boilers would increase *Nevada*'s cruising radius, a key factor given ongoing concerns about potential conflict with Japan in the Pacific.

To complete the makeover of *Nevada*'s machinery, new propellers were designed. The Bureau of Engineering was determined to maximize fuel efficiency by using the most advanced propeller design available. Engineers validated the new design through tests on scale models of *Oklahoma*'s hull (nearly identical to *Nevada*'s) in the Navy's model basin in Washington.

Above the main deck, *Nevada* received a completely new look. The Navy had received numerous complaints about hull-mounted secondary armament becoming wet and unusable in heavy seas. Some of the 5-inch guns had been removed before *Nevada* sailed for Europe in World War I. Now, the remaining ones were taken out, and ten of them were moved to a specially built deckhouse higher on the ship. The bridge and captain's quarters were rebuilt, and the smokestack was tilted slightly aft to make room for the new superstructure and the tripod-design foremast.

While the battleship still reigned supreme in naval warfare, the Navy understood the implications of Billy Mitchell's demonstration of sinking a battleship with air-delivered bombs. In response, eight 5-inch antiaircraft guns were added to *Nevada*'s battery, and additional antiaircraft machine guns were placed atop the fire control stations on each mast, significantly enhancing her air defense capabilities.

The torpedo tubes on *Nevada* and *Oklahoma* sparked considerable discussion, since the new antitorpedo blister had rendered them unusable in their original position. The General Board initially recommended shifting the tubes from their original position below the waterline to the main deck. However, Lt. Cmdr. C. B. C. Carey of the Bureau of Ordnance challenged this recommendation, arguing that torpedoes on a ship's main deck

On a foggy September 5, 1929, *Nevada* looms ghostlike along Pier 4 at Norfolk Navy Yard. Her modernization had cost approximately $3 million (equivalent to approximately $5.5 billion in current dollars). *National Archives*

Nevada is departing from the Norfolk Navy Yard upon completion of her modernization, on September 9, 1929. She was headed to sea for a monthlong shakedown cruise, to run speed trials and have her performance and seaworthiness evaluated.

were at risk of detonation by shell fragments or in a fire. He also pointed out that torpedoes were unlikely to be a factor in engagements between battleships, citing that not one of the twelve torpedoes that British capital ships fired in the Battle of Jutland hit its target. After considering Carey's memo, the General Board reversed its decision and recommended removing the torpedo tubes from *Nevada* and *Oklahoma* entirely.

The most significant change to *Nevada*'s offensive capability—increasing the maximum elevation of the guns from 15 degrees to 30 degrees—proved as challenging technically as it had been politically. New turret armor would have been prohibitively expensive, so engineers had to find a way to enlarge the openings in the existing 18-inch-thick armor faceplates.

Bethlehem Steel and Carnegie Steel Companies, the makers of the original armor, recommended preheating the armor to just above the boiling point of water and then using cutting torches to enlarge the openings. Grinders would then smooth the edges. However, Commandant Todd had reservations about this approach, concerned that cutting by torch would heat the armor and potentially change its hardness from the original demanding specifications.

Todd sought advice within the Norfolk Navy Yard and found an officer with experience cutting thick armor on the former German battleship *Helgoland*. Further information from the Bureau of Ordnance convinced Todd that torches were not the best solution. Instead, he suggested drilling closely spaced holes just inside the desired contour of the new gunports and using industrial grinders to finish the openings. The bureau was impressed with Todd's analysis and endorsed his approach.

Once approved, yard crews began the painstaking process of unbolting armor plates from the front of the turrets and positioning them on heavy timber cradles. Then, 30-ton jacks maneuvered the plates into position under a drill press fitted with a 1$^{3}/_{32}$-inch-diameter bit. By overlapping the holes during drilling, debris was ejected into the expanding cut, making the process faster. Still, with seventy-two holes required per opening and ten openings to cut, it was a lengthy and labor-intensive process.

To more efficiently move shells from the magazines to the guns, new powder and shell hoists were installed in the main turrets and the newly positioned 5-inch guns in the superstructure. The two-gun-turret magazines were configured to store 196 shells, and the three-gun-turret magazines could store 214 shells, providing a total of roughly forty-one ten-gun salvos.

The greatly increased range enabled by higher gun elevation meant that potential targets might be over the horizon, invisible even from the highest masts. To address this, two catapults were installed, one on the quarterdeck and one atop turret 3, and three Vought O2U-3 Corsair pontoon biplanes were provided as aerial spotters, significantly enhancing *Nevada*'s long-range targeting capabilities.

As the modernization progressed, crew comfort also received attention. When originally built, *Nevada* berthed enlisted men in hammocks, many of them slung in the 5-inch gun compartments along the sides of the ship. On July 23, 1928, Commandant Todd wrote to the Bureau of Construction and Repair that there was sufficient space to provide steel-pipe bunks for 1,053 men. Assuming a war complement of 1,440, that left only 387 to make do in hammocks. A peacetime crew of 1,269 would require only 216 men to sleep in the less comfortable hammocks.

The bureau initially replied that money was tight, and it could not authorize the shift to bunks. Todd persisted, arguing that most of the work was already done. The bureau's response was deliberately vague: "It is satisfactory to the Bureau for the Yard to consider this item as not now definitely disapproved." Taking this as tacit approval, Todd proceeded with the installation of bunks.

Capt. Royall then requested suitable mattresses, since those supplied for hammocks were too short and wide for the new bunks. He also suggested stocking mattress covers in the ship's clothing and small stores, so that men could buy their own. Taking a logical but unsympathetic tone, bureau manager Henry Williams responded that enlisted men were supposed to use their hammock mattresses regardless of whether they were berthed in hammocks or standee bunks. He noted that the short hammock mattresses "are supplemented with a pillow which is supposed to remedy the conditions mentioned." Williams closed by saying he would refer the whole matter to the commander in chief of the Battle Fleet, a not-so-subtle way of putting both Todd and Royall on notice for attempting to circumvent the system.

When Royall attempted to have the old lavatories in enlisted men's quarters—bench seats placed atop troughs leading over the side—replaced with modern enamel toilets, the bureau responded on October 17, 1928, disapproving the change. They argued that enamel scratched easily and would soon present an unhygienic appearance. Moreover, flush toilets would encourage crew members to use more water, a precious commodity at sea.

Interestingly, while denying Royall's request to improve the crew's facilities, the bureau did order the installation of eight "experimental" metal lavatories in officers' country. Perhaps as a form of bureaucratic payback for Royall's attempt to change the crew's arrangements, on March 5, 1929, the bureau wrote requiring that "the Commanding Officer should . . . submit reports, at six month intervals, covering the performance of these lavatories in service."

The galley and bakery were slated for a complete overhaul. One addition sure to delight the galley team was an automatic dishwasher/sterilizer. An industrial-size unit was required to handle three meals a day for more than 1,400 men, and the Navy chose one that was based on a conveyor system; dirty dishes entered on one side and emerged sparkling clean on the other. Numerous other galley items required attention, from refinishing messroom furniture to repairing the cake mixer. While the bureau politely refused Todd's suggestion to refinish the ship's silverware, he kept the project on his wish list and managed to fit it in by the end of the modernization.

Details of the aft part of USS *Nevada* following her modernization are viewed from the starboard side at Norfolk Navy Yard on September 5, 1929. Above the deck to the left is the catapult, and a new catapult has been mounted on top of turret 3. The indentation on the hull in the foreground marks the former location of a 5-inch gun casement. On the mainmast just above that catapult is a rangefinder. *National Archives National Archives*

Although the galley itself was modernized, the men continued to eat in their berthing compartments. A junior member of each group was tasked with collecting food from the galley, bread from the bakery, and plates and silverware from the pantry. Tables and benches were stored against the overhead and lowered on cables when needed, a space-saving measure that had long been standard practice on naval vessels.

As *Nevada* neared completion of her modernization, on December 3, 1929, the commander of Battleship Division 3 asked the Bureau of Construction and Repair to temporarily install quarters suitable for a flag officer aboard the ship. His usual flagship, *New York*, was in the yard, and he wasn't satisfied with the inferior quarters of a mere ship commander. The Chief of Naval Operations made a special effort to express his disapproval of this request, seeing it as an unnecessary luxury during a time of budget constraints.

Nevada's completion date was originally scheduled for April 30, 1929, but by February of that year, it had already slipped to June 29. Norfolk's May 18, 1929, weekly progress report noted that only 76.6 percent of the work was done, and while the outer superstructure was complete, interior compartments were still under construction. Completion was pushed back further following the August 17 progress report, which noted that some of the most important remaining work had to do with ordnance—the trunnions holding the guns in the triple turrets were only half done.

This story of delays was reminiscent of *Nevada*'s original construction—an optimistic early completion date marred by unforeseen problems. But this time, the Navy was doing the work at its own yard; there was no private contractor to blame for the delays. The good news was that the work done by the Norfolk Navy Yard came in $43,654.27 under budget, despite Commandant Todd and Capt. Royall adding crew bunks, silverware replating, and other comforts to the work list.

As for the delay, Commandant Todd had already protected himself in January 1929 when he wrote to the Bureaus of Construction and Repair and Engineering complaining that late delivery of plans and a lack of draftsmen were putting his schedule at risk. Todd, a veteran of the Navy's bureaucracy, knew how to navigate the system and preemptively deflect blame.

As Todd's punch list shortened, new crew members began to arrive on board, many from *Arizona*, which had recently arrived at the yard for her own major rebuild. On June 1, 1929, *Nevada* was transferred from what was essentially inactive status to Battleship Division 3 of the Scouting Fleet, and on August 1 she was placed back in full commission. Still to come were the sea trials—a retake of nearly all the tests she underwent before her first commissioning, not surprising since she was essentially a new ship.

By September 5, 1929, there were 1,077 sailors on board *Nevada* and a full complement of officers and Marines—she was ready for sea. At 0905, three tugs stood by to nudge the ship from the pier into the channel, and at 0920 both main engines were tested. The tugs waited patiently, but at 1032 Capt. Royall canceled *Nevada*'s departure due to a failure in the always-problematic steering telemotor. Workers disassembled the unit and remade several parts overnight. *Nevada* finally left the pier at 1030 the next morning, beginning a new chapter in her service life.

Gun trials were conducted at the Navy's range at Dahlgren, Virginia. The ship moored at a set of buoys off Piney Point Lighthouse and fired at a predefined location near Smith Point, 31,500 yards away. One pilot shot was permitted before five full salvos. The shells contained brightly colored dyes so that the splashes from individual turrets could be distinguished from one

USS *Nevada* is observed from the forward-port quarter at the Norfolk Navy Yard on September 6, 1929. The searchlight platforms on both cage masts had been replaced by search platforms on the sides of the smokestack and on the superstructure. Two additional 3-inch antiaircraft guns had been installed on each side of the superstructure deck, near the boat cranes. *National Archives*

another. The primary objective of these tests was to study shell dispersion—the tightness of a salvo pattern—at extreme range. A secondary objective was to set the air pressure in the counterrecoil mechanisms of the guns when firing at maximum elevation. This marked the first time that *Nevada*'s 14-inch guns had been fired at ranges beyond about 20,000 yards, a significant milestone in her modernization.

In addition to the long-range gunnery tests, ten-gun salvos were fired with the guns at 0-degree elevation, the configuration most stressful to the ship's structure. Damage from these tests was relatively minor: a sprung door in the captain's pantry, some shattered portholes, and minor issues with the ship's boats. These results were encouraging, demonstrating that *Nevada*'s structure could withstand the stress of full broadsides even after her extensive modifications.

For her machinery and performance trials, *Nevada* returned to the Navy's measured mile off Rockland, Maine. As in the builder's trials in 1915, the Navy laid down very specific requirements for the tests, starting with total displacement. The Washington Naval Treaty decreed that modifications to a capital ship could add no more than 3,000 tons to her displacement, and since *Nevada* was commissioned at 27,500 tons, she would do her second set of trials at exactly 30,500 tons. The bureau mandated that the draft of the ship would be 28 feet, 8 inches.

However, someone had miscalculated. Capt. Royall promptly wrote back that *Nevada* could not reach the specified displacement and draft unless he unloaded 1,000 tons of fuel and ammunition, a process that could take eight days and might leave the ship with insufficient fuel to conduct the trials and return to Boston. Without admitting any mistake, the bureau instructed *Nevada* to conduct trials with the ammunition and fuel on board, using the excuse that normal displacement was 30,500 tons and that the ship just happened to have extra material on board. This bureaucratic sleight of hand allowed the trials to proceed without delay.

Performance trials got underway at 0616 on Wednesday, October 26, 1929. The weather was clear, with a moderate chop on the sea, acceptable conditions for testing the ship's new hull profile and power plant. In twenty standardization runs on a measured mile, *Nevada* reached a respectable top speed of 20.38 knots, only 0.12 knots slower than her 1916 specifications despite the added water resistance associated with the antitorpedo blisters. However, the change in hull design with the addition of the blisters was found to make her unwieldy at slow speeds, a trade-off for improved protection.

Over the next several days, the board's inspectors put *Nevada* through her paces. On Thursday morning, she conducted a four-hour economy trial at 15 knots, using four of her six boilers. In the afternoon, it was the same but at full power, with all boilers online. *Nevada* burned more than 18 tons of fuel per hour at full speed. However, the boilers smoked excessively at any speed above 19 knots, indicating a poor air-to-fuel ratio in the burners—a problem that would need addressing.

After the full-power trial, course was set for the Virginia Capes, where a third four-hour trial was conducted, this one at

The tugboat *Hercules* is assisting the newly modernized *Nevada* as she moves along the channel off Norfolk Navy Yard on September 6, 1930. Much of the crew is present on the weather decks. A comparison of this photo with premodernization photos of *Nevada* reveals a number of prominent changes to the superstructure. *National Archives*

The starboard side of *Nevada* is seen in silhouette at Norfolk Navy Yard on September 6, 1929. During modernization, changes had been made to the boat cranes, which now had long booms extending from the tops of the king posts, supported by substantial braces. *National Archives*

10 knots, with less than 4 tons of fuel consumed per hour. Next came punishing reversing tests. *Nevada* worked her way up to full speed, and Captain Royall ordered full reverse. During the two minutes and forty-five seconds it took the ship to stop, she covered 745 yards. From full speed astern, it took one minute and forty-five seconds to stop over a distance of 266 yards, demonstrating the ship's improved maneuverability and stopping power.

The trials were largely a success, but just as in the original runs in 1915–16, various small problems surfaced with the new machinery. A feed pump blew a gasket, a condenser in the dynamo room sprung a leak, and a fuel pump malfunctioned. On the positive side, the new engines performed brilliantly. At 10 knots, *Nevada* could now steam 13,530 miles, compared to 8,950 miles using her original engines. At nearly full speed, she could push 6,140 miles compared with only 2,780 miles with her original equipment. In terms of mileage, at the economical speed of 10 knots, *Nevada* covered about 4.5 miles per ton of fuel, or about 50 feet per gallon—a significant improvement in fuel efficiency.

While the machinery performed well, the board was less impressed with the men operating it. The report noted that "the Engineer's force was not yet sufficiently efficient to obtain the results that should have been expected on the fuel consumption trials." This observation highlighted the need for intensive training to bring the crew up to speed with *Nevada*'s new systems and capabilities.

As *Nevada* completed her trials and prepared to rejoin the fleet, she emerged as a ship reborn. The extensive modernization had transformed her from an aging warship struggling with reliability issues into a formidable battleship equipped with the latest technology. Her increased gun range, improved protection, and enhanced fuel efficiency made her a valuable asset to the US Navy as it faced the uncertainties of the 1930s.

The modernization of *Nevada* represented more than just an upgrade to a single ship; it was a testament to the Navy's commitment to maintaining a powerful and relevant battle fleet within the constraints of interwar treaties and budget limitations. The innovative solutions employed in her refit—from the repurposing of *North Dakota*'s engines to the clever work-arounds for treaty restrictions—showcased American naval engineering prowess and adaptability.

As *Nevada* steamed out to rejoin the fleet, she carried with her the hopes and expectations of a Navy preparing for an uncertain future. The lessons learned from her modernization would inform future upgrades and new ship designs, ensuring that the US Navy remained at the forefront of naval technology and capability. *Nevada*'s transformation from an aging warrior to a thoroughly modern battleship was complete, setting the stage for her crucial role in the years to come.

CHAPTER 5

Return to the Fleet

Nevada's return to fleet service was delayed until January 4, 1930, due to a broken deck lug on one of the guns in turret 3. After two and a half years in the yard, she departed Norfolk bound for Guantánamo as a unit of Battleship Division 3 (BatDiv3), under the command of Capt. Hilary H. Royall. From Cuba, she conducted battle practice off Panama before steaming to New York. On May 7, 1930, *Nevada* participated in a presidential review for President Herbert Hoover off Hampton Roads.

On June 10, *Nevada* transited the Panama Canal, returning to the Pacific and her home port at San Pedro. The canal passage proved eventful, since her notorious rudder problems recurred, exacerbated by poor slow-speed handling due to the addition of torpedo blisters. At one point, following a steering casualty, *Nevada* was perpendicular to the canal channel, trailing 165 fathoms of anchor chain. Her starboard bow blister was damaged entering the Pedro Miguel Locks, and two hours later she hit the Miraflores Locks with her midships port blister. After finally clearing the canal, she endured the further embarrassment of losing her starboard anchor.

These mishaps necessitated repairs at Puget Sound, after which *Nevada* made a summer cruise in the Pacific Northwest, calling at various ports. She returned to San Pedro on August 26, 1930, and remained there until February 5, 1931, save for a brief sortie to San Francisco in November.

Throughout 1931, *Nevada* conducted multiple sorties from San Pedro, making periodic port visits along the California coast. She served as host to the 1931 Secondary Battery Gunnery School, with her secondary batteries firing upward of two hundred rounds per day. On December 4, she participated in a shore bombardment exercise on San Clemente Island, simulating support for an amphibious landing—a prescient training for her future role.

The year 1932 saw *Nevada* participating in Fleet Problem XIII in Hawaiian waters from February to March. She then alternated between periods in port and coastal cruises, conducting training and making port visits. In December, she entered Puget Sound Navy Yard for repairs and modifications, including the installation of eight .50-caliber antiaircraft machine guns and regunning of her main and secondary batteries.

Nevada spent much of 1933 operating along the California coast, with periodic returns to San Pedro and visits to San Francisco. A somber event occurred on November 12, when RAdm. Ridley McLean, commander of BatDiv3, died suddenly from a heart attack aboard *Nevada*, the division flagship, while anchored in San Francisco Bay. Funeral services were held on board the next day.

In early 1934, *Nevada* underwent another overhaul at Puget Sound. Engineers addressed her postmodernization problem of poor handling at slow speeds, determining that the torpedo blister was diverting water away from the rudder. The Bureau of Construction and Repair ordered the installation of a "deadwood" section between the rudder and the curve of the stern, which successfully solved the handling issue. Plumbing was also added to allow *Nevada* to refuel destroyers while underway, enhancing her escort capabilities.

From April to May 1934, *Nevada* participated in Fleet Problem XV in the Caribbean. She then returned to the Pacific, undergoing repairs at Puget Sound Navy Yard in June. The latter part of the year saw her conducting training exercises and making port visits along the West Coast and in the Panama Canal Zone.

In 1935, *Nevada* was involved in search-and-rescue operations for survivors of the airship *Macon* (ZRS-5), which crashed off Monterey Bay on February 12. Later that year, from April 29 to June 10, she participated in Fleet Problem XVI in Hawaiian waters, the largest such exercise held in the Pacific to date. This problem was the first to incorporate four aircraft carriers and evaluate the fleet's abilities in various aspects of a naval campaign.

The year 1936 began with another overhaul at Puget Sound Navy Yard, including regunning of her secondary battery. From May to June, *Nevada* took part in Fleet Problem XVII in the Gulf of Panama, which simulated a Japanese surprise attack on Pearl Harbor. During part of this exercise, *Nevada* had to steam on only her port engine due to a leaky starboard condenser.

In 1937, *Nevada* participated in Fleet Problem XVIII from April to May, spending time at Pearl Harbor and San Francisco. She underwent another overhaul at Puget Sound Navy Yard from July to November.

March 1938 saw *Nevada* bound for Hawaiian waters to engage in Fleet Problem XIX. This exercise, like Fleet Problem XVI, was set in the Pacific Triangle—the North American West Coast, Hawaii, and the Aleutian Islands. Despite *Nevada* spotting the attacking Blue force aircraft the day before the "attack," these sightings were dismissed. VAdm. Ernest King managed to get his carriers within 100 miles of Oahu before launching a mock attack on Pearl Harbor, Hickam Field, and Wheeler Field. Although

Nevada is standing at anchor off Naval Air Station Coco Solo, in the Canal Zone, on February 12, 1930. An observation plane is mounted on each catapult, and a third aircraft is on the deck next to turret 3. Three aircraft was the normal complement for battleships in the 1930s. *National Archives*

This photograph of USS *Nevada* was inscribed on the negative with a photo number and "2-30," which presumably indicates it was taken in February 1930. Indeed, features of the ship in the photo indicate it was taken some time between September 1929, when her modernization (including the tripod masts) was completed, and 1934, by which time the new, lattice-design aircraft crane had been mounted. Three observation planes are aboard: one on the catapult on turret 3 and two on the aft catapult. They appear to be either Vought O2Us or O3Us. *National Archives*

A photographer on an aircraft from USS *Saratoga* (CV-3) took this view of *Nevada* with her main-battery guns trained to starboard, during fleet maneuvers out of Guantánamo on March 24, 1930. A Vought O2U-3 Corsair observation plane is mounted on each catapult. *National Archives*

In a photograph taken from a plane from the carrier USS *Saratoga* (CV-3), the main battery of USS *Nevada* is trained to starboard during fleet maneuvers off Guantánamo Bay, Cuba, on March 24, 1930. Stored on the side of turret 1 is a paravane. The observation plane on the turret 3 catapult has the side number "3/6." *National Archives*

referees declared that the strike had inflicted heavy damage, superior officers discounted King's strategy as a lucky hit aided by weather.

Later in 1938, *Nevada*, along with *Arizona* and *Pennsylvania*, was assigned to Battleship Division 1 (BatDiv1). Each ship received three Curtiss SOC Seagull aircraft, forming observation squadron VO-1B. In October the Bureau of Inspection and Survey examined *Nevada*, concluding that while no serious defects were noted, the ship was in many respects obsolescent. The report questioned the advisability of piecemeal improvements and recommended considering reclassifying *Nevada* as other than a first-line battleship.

Throughout 1939, *Nevada* continued her routine of maintenance, training exercises, and port visits. During her January overhaul at Puget Sound Navy Yard, concerns were raised about the watertight integrity of compartments on the second and third decks, some of which lacked watertight hatches. However, correcting this would have involved significant unauthorized expenditure.

The year 1940 saw *Nevada* participating in Fleet Problem XXI, the last to be executed, from April 1 through May 17. She continued to operate off the West Coast and in Hawaiian waters throughout the year, entering Puget Sound Navy Yard for her regular maintenance period in November.

On February 25, 1941, *Nevada* left Puget Sound Navy Yard for Long Beach, California. On March 2, her Seagulls were replaced by Vought OS2U-3 Kingfisher aircraft. She then set course for her new home port at Pearl Harbor, arriving on March 25. As tensions with Japan increased, she spent much of her time conducting training in the waters between Hawaii and the West Coast. The intensity of training increased, with battleships often at sea for ten days at a time, a stark contrast to earlier years, when ships would ride at anchor for months.

On November 29, *Nevada* and *Arizona* steamed from Pearl Harbor with *Enterprise*, joined by *Oklahoma* the next day. Unlike previous training operations, this was a ruse intended to mask *Enterprise*'s high-speed delivery of fighters to Wake Island. The ruse was cut short by reports of Japanese submarines near Oahu, and the three battleships were recalled to Pearl Harbor.

At 0800 on Saturday, December 6, as *Nevada* entered the channel, her secondary and antiaircraft batteries were manned, a practice that had become standard Navy procedure earlier in the year due to concerns of a surprise attack. Harbor entry was uneventful, and tugs shoved the aging dreadnought tight against Berth F-8, the northernmost mooring quay in Pearl Harbor's battleship row.

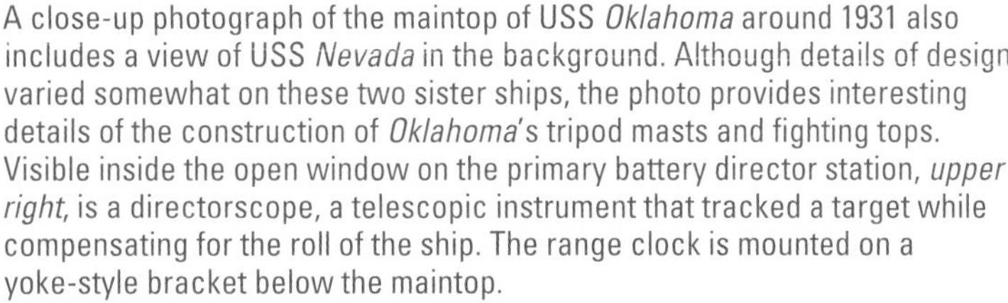

A close-up photograph of the maintop of USS *Oklahoma* around 1931 also includes a view of USS *Nevada* in the background. Although details of design varied somewhat on these two sister ships, the photo provides interesting details of the construction of *Oklahoma*'s tripod masts and fighting tops. Visible inside the open window on the primary battery director station, *upper right*, is a directorscope, a telescopic instrument that tracked a target while compensating for the roll of the ship. The range clock is mounted on a yoke-style bracket below the maintop.

Nevada is entering Dry Dock 1 at Pearl Harbor, for maintenance and inspections, on February 15, 1932. Periodic drydockings were necessary to keep the lower hull scraped of marine growths and painted. *National Archives*

Work is underway on *Nevada* in Dry Dock 1, Pearl Harbor Navy Yard, on March 6, 1932. Men on staging planks are scraping and inspecting the hull below the waterline. Below and aft of the raised anchor is the forward end of the antitorpedo blister, which was installed during the ship's modernization. The blister formed an extra shell outside the original hull, designed to detonate or weaken the impact of torpedo hits along the vital machinery spaces. *Naval History and Heritage Command*

Nevada's battleship number, 36, is painted in a light color on the roof of turret 2 in this photo of the ship near the Pedro Miguel Locks of the Panama Canal on April 23, 1934. Locomotives called mules, on tracks on the pier, towed ships while in the locks. *National Archives*

Another photo from April 23, 1934, shows *Nevada* in the Pedro Miguel Locks. One of the imperatives of US capital ship planning and construction was that the ships' width had to fit within the locks of the Panama Canal. Two submarines are in the channel next to *Nevada*'s. *National Archives*

Nevada is at anchor off Colón, Canal Zone, around June 1934. White blast bags are fitted over the barrels of the 14-inch guns where they enter the turrets. The black-colored shapes on the forecastle are chafing plates, to protect the wooden deck from the rubbing of the anchor chains. *National Archives*

Nevada is docked at Puget Sound Navy Yard, Bremerton, Washington, in September 1934. A white "E" award for excellence in gunnery is faintly visible on turret 1, near the far left. A paravane is stored farther aft on that turret. Below the paravane, on the rail, is a "USS NEVADA" name plate. Several crewmen are touching up paint on the side of the pilothouse and the underside of the rangefinder platform above the navigating bridge. *Naval History and Heritage Command*

Nevada General Data, 1929	
Dimensions	
Length overall	583'0"
Waterline length	575'0"
Maximum beam	107'11"
Deep draft	29'7"
Rebuilder	Norfolk Naval Shipyard
Entered shipyard	January 2, 1928
Left shipyard	June 1, 1929
Recommissioned	August 1, 1929
Displacement	
30,500 tons standard	
33,901 tons design emergency	
Armor Protection	
Belt	13.5" tapering to 8", 17'4⅝" wide, 8'6" below water
Armor deck	80 lb. STS + 50 lb. STS + 50 lb. STS + 20 lb.; aft 180 lb. STS + 70 lb. amidships
Splinter deck	40 lb. NS + 20 lb. / 60 lb NS + 20 lb. STS + 20 lb. / 60 lb. STS + 20 lb.
Turrets	
Faceplates	18"; sides: 16"/5" STS / 10"–9"
Barbettes	
13" above second deck, 5" between second and half decks	
Conning Tower	
16" + 50 lb. STS / 5" STS	
Armament	
Main battery	10 14"/45
Secondary battery	12 5"/51
AA battery	8 5"/25 + 8 .50 BMG
Machinery	
Boilers	6 Bureau Express 300 psi
Engines	2 geared turbines
Shaft horsepower	25,000 maximum ahead
Maximum speed	20.5 knots
Endurance	12 knots: 5,195 nautical miles
Rudders	1, balanced
Fuel	3,148 tons oil

Possibly taken from a crane at Puget Sound Navy Yard, this view takes in *Nevada* from turret 3, *lower right*, to the bow. Also visible in the preceding photograph is a newly installed machine gun platform, perched above the maintop. This was fitted with four .50-caliber machine guns on pedestal mounts. *Naval History and Heritage Command*

Turrets 1, 2, and 4 are trained to starboard as USS *Nevada* is underway around the spring of 1935. Three Vought O3U-3 observation planes are spotted on the catapults. The sides of the bridge still have six windows; these would be increased to nine by August 1935. The ship's battleship number, 36, is visible on the roof of turret 2. *National Archives*

USS *Nevada* is at anchor off San Pedro, California, on April 22, 1935. The upper half of the mainmast was painted black, to mask the soot that collected on it from the smokestack. The top of the smokestack also was painted black. *National Archives*

The black paint on the upper half of the mainmast is also readily apparent in this photo of *Nevada* underway at sea in August 1935. Recently the original aircraft crane on the stern was replaced by a much-sturdier crane. It is seen here folded down to the deck. A noticeable change to the ship since the April 22, 1935, photo was the addition of steel plating and windows to the previously open area at the rear of the bridge: Previously, there were six windows on each side of the bridge, and now there were nine. *National Archives*

This undated photo of USS *Nevada* contains several clues as to when the photo was taken. The three aircraft embarked are Vought O3U-3s, and these aircraft were assigned to *Nevada* by June 1933, continuing to serve on the ship until sometime between September 1937 and July 1938. The navigating bridge has nine windows on the side, a feature dating to around August 1935. The smokestack appears in its original height, before being extended in height by April 1936. Hence, the photo probably dates to between August 1935 and April 1936. *National Archives*

A view of *Nevada* in drydock at Pearl Harbor around 1935 provides details of the bulbous bow. On the bottom of the bow is a protrusion with two holes in it; the paravane chains (which have been temporarily removed) were routed through these openings. Toward the right is the lowered anchor. *Naval History and Heritage Command*

A freshly repainted USS *Nevada* is moored to a dock at Puget Yard Navy Yard in April 1936. The outer part of the booms of the boat cranes had been painted black: This feature is visible in some of the 1935 photos of the ship. An "E" award has been painted at the top of the smokestack. Recently the height of the smokestack had been increased noticeably. Now, the tops of the searchlights on the sides of the smokestack, which previously had been nearly level with the top of the stack, were considerably lower with reference to the top. *Puget Sound Naval Shipyard*

The Golden Gate Bridge, still under construction, looms over four US battleships departing San Francisco Bay for the Pacific Ocean around November 1936. *From left to right*: USS *Arizona* (BB-39), USS *Nevada*, USS *Maryland* (BB-46), and USS *Texas* (BB-35). *Naval History and Heritage Command*

Nevada is underway at sea in an undated photograph. The heightened smokestack, dating from 1936, is present, but the black paint on the mainmast, present in 1935 and 1936, has been painted over in gray. The large, cloverleaf searchlight platform installed on the mainmast by April 1939 is not yet present. Hence, it seems likely this photo was taken around 1937–38. *National Archives*

Nevada was photographed at the Puget Sound Navy Yard on April 21, 1939. The ship has the appearance of having been repainted, and the upper half of the mainmast, previously painted black, was now the same shade of light gray as the rest of the ship. *Puget Sound Naval Shipyard*

A photo of *Nevada* off her port-aft quarter probably dates to between 1939, by which time the enlarged "cloverleaf" searchlight platform was added to the mainmast, and February 1941, when the spare anchor on the port side was eliminated and the portholes on the forward hull were plugged. Above turret 2 is the mainmast and maintop of another battleship.

USS *Nevada* is thought to have been in this battle group, on maneuvers in the Pacific in mid-September 1940. USS *Arizona* (BB-39) was also among this number. Flying above the force are a formation of Douglas TBD torpedo bombers followed by Northrop BT dive-bombers.

USS *Nevada* again visited the Puget Sound Navy Yard in early 1941 and is seen in a photo dated February 19. Portholes on the forward part of the hull had just been removed and the openings plugged; some of these plugs have been covered with a dark-colored primer. The locations of other plugs appear as squares that are slightly darker than the surrounding gray paint. A splinter shield had been installed on the platform on the foremast above the bridge. *Puget Sound Naval Shipyard*

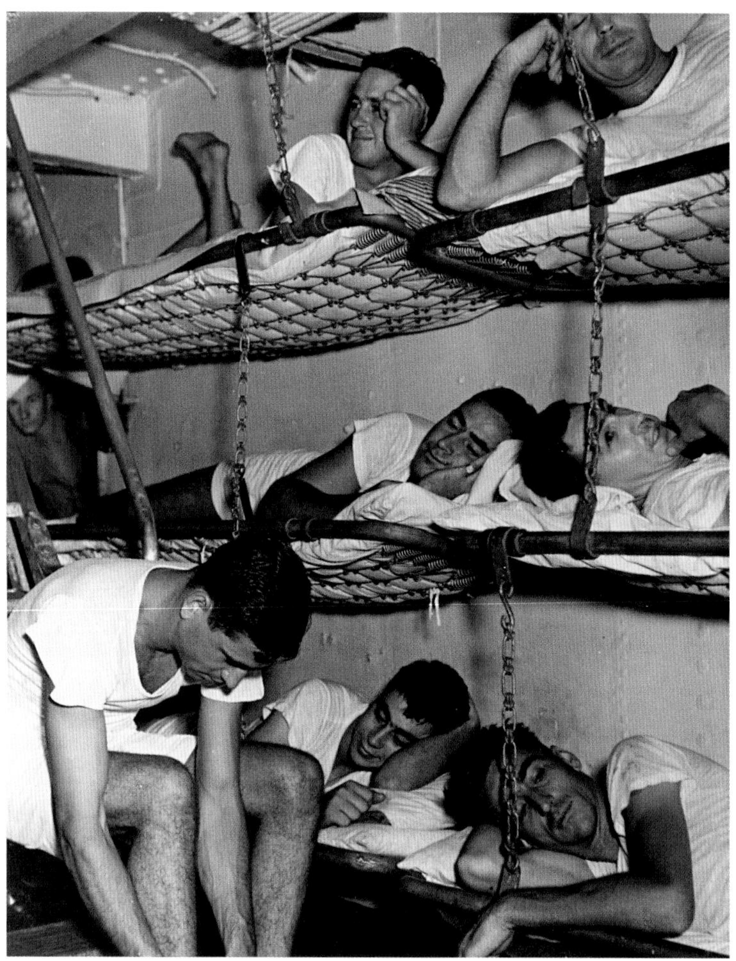

Seven Patten brothers, Allen, Ray, Myrne, Clarence Jr., Gilbert, Bruce, and Marvin, served on USS *Nevada* just before the Pearl Harbor attack, and they are shown in a corner where they berthed together around September 9, 1941. On that day, their father, Clarence Patten Sr., enlisted in the Navy so he could join his sons on *Nevada*. *Naval History and Heritage Command*

CHAPTER 6

Pearl Harbor

At 0350 on December 7, 1941, the coastal minesweeper *Condor* (AMc-14) spotted a submarine periscope less than 2 miles from the harbor entrance. *Condor* promptly alerted the destroyer *Ward* (DD-139) at 0357: "Sighted submerged submarine on westerly course, speed 9 knots." This crucial message was picked up by the naval radio station at Bishop's Point but went unnoticed by the Fourteenth Naval District communications watch due to a sleeping lieutenant.

Ward conducted a search but failed to establish contact, securing from General Quarters at 0435 while continuing to patrol. At 0458 the antitorpedo net boom was opened to allow *Condor* and *Crossbill* to return to harbor, with the general cargo ship *Antares* (AKS-3) expected at 0600.

At 0605, *Ward* made visual contact with *Antares*, an 11,000-ton vessel under Cmdr. Lawrence C. Grannis's command. *Antares*, towing a barge and returning from Canton, had experienced multiple possible submarine sightings during its transit. At 0630, *Antares* arrived off Pearl Harbor's entrance to transfer the barge to a tug. During a slow turn, lookouts spotted an object 1,500 yards on the starboard quarter, which Cmdr. Grannis quickly identified as a submarine.

Antares transmitted a clear message to *Ward* at 0637: "A partially submerged submarine spotted 1500 yards off starboard quarter . . . seems to be having depth control trouble . . . trying to go down." *Ward* responded, "Roger, *Antares*. Stand by."

Lt. William Outerbridge, *Ward*'s commanding officer, ordered General Quarters at 0640. By 0645, *Ward* had closed to within 300 yards of the submarine. At about 100 yards, *Ward*'s forward 4-inch gun fired, narrowly missing the submarine's conning tower. As the submarine passed down *Ward*'s side, the starboard 4-inch gun scored a direct hit at the base of the conning tower from just 50 yards.

Outerbridge ordered an immediate depth-charge attack as the submarine passed astern. Four "ashcans" set for a 100-foot depth were dropped, appearing to detonate under the submarine. The target rolled over and sank, never to resurface. The wreck of Japanese Ko-hyoteki-class submarine *HA-18*, with its conning tower holed by gunfire, was discovered in 2002, confirming *Ward*'s claim.

At 0653, Outerbridge sent a detailed message to Com 14: "USS *Ward* to Com 14. Have attacked, fired upon, and dropped depth-charges upon unidentified submarine operating in defensive sea area . . . a direct hit from our number three gun on his conning tower. Followed up with four ashcans. Oil slick 300 yards astern visible on surface—Lt. William W Outerbridge, CO USS *Ward* (DD-139)."

It wasn't until 0712 that the Fourteenth Naval District was notified. Adm. Claude C. Bloch, district commandant, ordered the submarine net closed and the ready duty destroyer to sea, also notifying Fleet Cmdr. Husband Kimmel's duty officer, Cmdr. Vincent Murphy.

Meanwhile, aboard *Nevada*, the crew was preparing for a routine Sunday. Many were eating breakfast, recovering from the previous day's ammunition unloading. With most senior officers ashore for the weekend, Lt. Cmdr. Francis J. Thomas, a naval reservist who had joined in June, was in command.

On deck, chaplains prepared for morning services, scheduled to begin shortly after colors at 0800. *Nevada*'s twenty-three-man band was ready to play the national anthem as the flag was raised. The 5-inch-gun crews had begun their daily fire control system checks, with ammunition ready boxes unlocked for the daily temperature check.

At 0755 the first Japanese bomb struck the seaplane ramp on Ford Island. RAdm. William Furlong, aboard the minelayer USS *Oglala*, recognized the Japanese markings and ordered General Quarters and the Emergency Sortie Plan into action. At 0758, RAdm. Patrick Bellinger radioed all ships: "AIR RAID PEARL HARBOR X THIS IS NOT DRILL."

On *Nevada*'s deck, just as the band began the "Star Spangled Banner," Ens. J. K. Taussig Jr., the officer of the deck and acting air defense officer, spotted a low-flying aircraft launching a torpedo. Taussig sounded the alarm and announced over the ship's public address system, "All hands, General Quarters. Air Raid! This is no drill."

Nevada's gunners, authorized earlier in the year to fire if under attack without further orders, opened fire at 0802. The .30-caliber machine guns on the searchlight platforms fired first, followed quickly by the .50-caliber and 5-inch guns.

At 0803, Chief Quartermaster Robert Sedberry ordered the engine room to prepare to get underway. Fortuitously, a second boiler was already being brought online to relieve the first. With Sedberry's order, fires were lit under the remaining boilers, except number 6, which was partially dismantled for maintenance.

Just before 8:00 a.m. on December 7, 1941, Japanese carrier-based aircraft attacked the US Fleet at Pearl Harbor. About ten minutes after the commencement of the attack, a Japanese torpedo struck the port side of USS *Nevada*, moored along Ford Island. The power plant was not damaged, and the engineering team of *Nevada* was able to raise sufficient steam to get the battleship underway by about 8:40 a.m. With the intention of making a run for the open sea, the crew navigated the damaged ship south down the harbor. She is seen here, with heavy smoke issuing from her, at around the time five Japanese bombs struck her, at about 9:00 a.m. The photo was taken from a water tower near the southeast shore of Ford Island; on the opposite side of *Nevada* is Ten Ten Dock and the 200-ton hammerhead crane in the Navy Yard. The small seaplane tender USS *Avocet* (AVP-4) is moored in the lower-right foreground. *Naval History and Heritage Command*

As steam was being raised, a Japanese Kate torpedo bomber struck *Nevada*'s port bow, opening a 16-by-27-foot hole. Lt. Cmdr. Thomas ordered four compartments starboard counterflooded to negate the list.

At 0820, Chief Boatswain Edwin Hill led a ten-man detail to swim to Quay F-9 and disconnect the securing lines. With steam rising, Lt. Cmdr. Thomas ordered Chief Quartermaster Sedberry to move the ship out. At 0840, *Nevada* began to back away from the quay, using her engines to steer since rudder control was minimal.

Nevada made her way down Battleship Row, attracting cheers from US servicemen and the attention of Japanese aviators, who saw an opportunity to sink her in the channel. Beginning at 0900, *Nevada* suffered five bomb hits in quick succession, three on the forecastle and two on the superstructure, causing fires and further damage.

Smoke from the fires entered the forward dynamo room. Warrant Officer Machinist Donald Ross ordered his men out but remained to keep the power on until overcome by smoke. After being rescued and revived, he dashed to the aft dynamo room, manning the equipment there until collapsing from heat exhaustion.

When *Nevada* was approximately abreast *California* in Berth F-3, orders were received not to leave the harbor. Lt. Cmdr. Thomas stopped the engines, intending to anchor near Hospital Point. Chief Boatswain Hill, who had gone forward to drop anchor, was killed along with other men when a bomb struck the forecastle, destroying the anchor gear.

As the situation became increasingly serious, Lt. Cmdr. Thomas sought to ground the ship between channel buoy 24 and the floating drydock. This is where *Nevada* rested when Capt. Scanland arrived by boat.

As the current began to break the ship free, with her stern pivoting out into the channel, Capt. Scanland, fearing that *Nevada* would block the channel, used two tugs to shove her stern first across the channel. He ordered full reverse at the last minute to securely ground the ship off Waipio Point. At 1045, *Nevada* came to rest on a coral shelf, her bow pointed south, listing 4 degrees to starboard and settling by the bow. Nevada's damage report noted:

> By about noon, water had entered the "bull ring"—i.e., the air intake and blower room surrounding the stack on the second deck, and the source of air for the forward part of the ship and all firerooms and started to flood the forward dynamo room through the ventilation trunk. Water extended on Sunday evening back to frame 80 on the second deck and was hip-deep at frame 50 (the "bull ring" extends between frames 56 and 76). Flooding on the third deck was checked at bulkhead 60 during the afternoon and at bulkhead 76 up until midnight.
>
> 14. The engineering plant went out of action unit by unit as water poured into the firerooms through the air intakes in the "bull ring." Boiler rooms 1, 2, 3, and 4 had been secured by 2330, but No. 6 boiler, which had been under overhaul, was reassembled and lit off at 2330. At about 0730 on December 8, No. 5 boiler room had to be secured, and the after pump room was flooding so rapidly that the last boiler room, No. 6 was abandoned. The loss of light and power added greatly to the difficulties in checking the flooding. Perhaps the tugs might have given pumping assistance, but it must have appeared a hopeless task; and in any case, the tugs seem to have been engaged in fighting the fires which were still burning on Monday.
>
> 15. Flooding continued all day Monday, and at nightfall the stern slipped off the coral ledge. The ship finally settled with a list of about two degrees to starboard and the main deck forward about four feet underwater. At high tide the main deck was dry only abaft frame 90 starboard and frame 75 port. The drafts were 48 feet forward and 39-1/2 feet aft. NEVADA remained in this position for over two months. Slow flooding continued for weeks, as evidenced by air bubbling up the trunks, and only a couple of compartments were found incompletely flooded when the ship was finally salvaged.
>
> Gasoline was forced up from the tank ruptured by bomb No. 2. It is believed that vapor collected forward of bulkhead 8-1/2 on the main deck. The fire already raging in the officers' country must have caused the vapor explosion which occurred on Sunday afternoon, and which resulted in more structural damage on the main and upper decks. There may have been intermittent minor vapor explosions. It was late Monday afternoon before this fire was extinguished. It was extremely stubborn, re-igniting when apparently out. The two forward bomb holes and a long split in the upper deck were stuffed with mattresses, and the fire was finally brought under control by smothering with steam supplied from the tugs.

Hearkening back to the October 1938 Bureau of Inspection and Survey report, the December 7 damage report concluded that "the damage which the enemy inflicted on this ship was comparatively superficial. The main machinery was not affected and most of the armament could continue in action. The ship sank because of deficiencies in watertight integrity, by virtue of the lack of watertight bulkheads on the second deck and failures of boundaries and fittings elsewhere which should have been watertight but were

Billowing smoke from burning ships frames USS *Nevada* as she makes her dash south down the channel at Pearl Harbor. The battleship is noticeably down at the bow. The huge gantry crane at the drydocks is to the left. *National Archives*

not. These converted a fairly simple repair job into a salvage and overhaul problem."

With her dynamo rooms flooded, *Nevada* began to receive electricity from the tug *Turkey*.

An initial count of the crew revealed the human toll: 29 men killed, 109 wounded, and 17 missing. At 1600 on December 7, 1941, in a somber moment amid the chaos, the colors were lowered to half-mast, and the dead were removed from the ship. Despite the considerable damage inflicted upon *Nevada*, her grounding during the attack had inadvertently ensured that she could be repaired and returned to action.

Among the battleships at Pearl Harbor, *Nevada*'s condition was relatively favorable. The *Pennsylvania*, which had been in drydock during the attack, was the least damaged. *Tennessee* and *Maryland*, moored inboard, had weathered the onslaught in good shape but were pinned by their sunken berth mates. Incredibly, despite her damage, *Nevada* was in the next-best condition.

The task of salvaging *Nevada* fell to forty-four-year-old Lt. Emile C. Genereaux. A reservist with extensive salvage expertise, Genereaux had been offered a commission by the Navy in early 1941 and called for active duty in August. When the Japanese struck, he had been assigned to the salvage base at San Diego. Ordered to Hawaii, Genereaux arranged to have his equipment shipped to Oahu on the troopship *Harris* before hitching a ride to Pearl Harbor on Secretary Knox's aircraft. Accompanying him was his executive officer, a reserve lieutenant (j.g.) from the Civil Engineer Corps named George M. Ankers.

Initially, there was hope to have *Nevada* refloated and in drydock by January 10, 1942, but this optimistic timeline proved unrealistic. Over five hundred dives were made on *Nevada* to survey underwater damage and prepare for refloating. Salvage experts calculated that 10,400 tons of water would need to be removed for the ship to be moved across the channel to Dry Dock 2.

Divers meticulously explored *Nevada*'s hull, recording the location and size of the holes. In an innovative approach, other salvors measured the hull of *Nevada*'s capsized sister ship, *Oklahoma*, to fabricate a massive wooden temporary patch for the largest opening—the wound caused by the torpedo striking near the bow.

Ankers took a creative approach to staffing the salvage operation. He arranged for members of *Nevada*'s crew, who knew her compartments and passageways intimately, to receive a brief course in diving. These men were tasked with descending inside

Nevada has steamed farther down the channel, her superstructure and forward hull being engulfed in smoke and flames. In the foreground is USS *Avocet*, on the water between her and *Nevada* is a pipeline to a dredge out in the harbor. *National Archives*

In a view from the same perspective as in the preceding photo, fires from bomb hits have enveloped the forward part of *Nevada* in flames. The ship was now crosswise in the channel, her stern jutting out toward the dredge line. *National Archives*

Nevada, backlit in a view looking toward the morning sun, continues smoking from the bomb strikes, as smoke also issues from her smokestack. *National Archives*

The battleship is proceeding south alongside the dredge line. Smoke and fires are centered on the superstructure and the smokestack. *National Archives*

the dark ship to secure watertight doors, close valves, and isolate oil tanks. Others detailed to the salvage crew waded through the 4-foot-deep water on the main deck to retrieve loose equipment, burned furniture, wrecked lockers, and clothing.

Throughout the first weeks of the salvage effort, Genereaux and Ankers reported steady progress to their superiors. The patching work was proceeding according to plan, and they maintained hope of delivering *Nevada* to the yard by January 10. On December 19, a hole in the bow made by an exiting bomb, located beneath the waterline at the second-deck level, was sealed with a 4-foot-square patch. Two days later, divers discovered two more ruptures in the bow: a gash several feet long and high on the port side at frame 7, and another on the starboard side at frame 13, where the corner had been pushed in 3 feet.

The fabrication of patches for these new holes began immediately aboard the repair ship *Medusa*, while divers from *Widgeon* trimmed the ragged edges. However, progress was hampered by several factors: the restriction of work to daylight hours due to blackout requirements, insufficient manpower to organize another shift, and a lack of transport to and from the ships. The salvage team was fortunate, though, that the removal of fire control equipment and guns had not been added to their duties—*Nevada* might need her armament soon.

By Christmas Day, Ankers reported that the fuel tanks inboard of the torpedo hole had been filled with carbon dioxide as a precaution against fire. The persistent delay in preparing the large patch for the torpedo hole remained a concern. Finally, on December 28, Ankers was advised that it would be ready on New Year's Eve. Rigging for the patch was sent out to *Nevada* the next day, and downhauls and A-frames were installed on the forecastle to hold the patch while divers positioned it.

As 1942 dawned, progress continued. On January 3, salvage crews rigged slings and shackles to secure the big patch, and five 10-inch centrifugal pumps were brought aboard to dewater the ship. The big patch was brought alongside *Nevada* at 0900 on January 8 by the tug *Gaylord*. However, a new challenge emerged: The patch could not be put into place because the portion projecting under the bow was hitting mud. For the next two days, efforts were made to siphon away the mud and coral to make way for the patch.

Meanwhile, even more pumps had been put aboard and had managed to lower the water level in *Nevada* by 9 inches. By January 12, the water level had dropped to just below the second deck. The once-pristine ship was filled with trash and filth—rotting food stores, enough to feed a thousand men for weeks, created an overwhelming stench. Clothing, paperwork, and bedding were

Although the ship is burning and considerably down at the bow, *Nevada*'s gun crews continue to man their weapons (*to the left*). One of the bombs that hit *Nevada* at around 9:00 a.m. struck immediately forward of the smokestack and exploded belowdecks. *National Archives*

water-soaked and usually ruined. Fuel oil and mud covered everything, and the final cleaning was done by hand, using rags.

Seating the big patch on *Nevada* proved more troublesome and time consuming than anticipated. By January 14, Ankers reported that the forward end was nearly in place, with the aft end 7 feet out from the hull. That gap was narrowed to just 1 foot the next day. Suction lines were being snaked throughout the second deck forward, and more discharge lines threw brown water and sludge over the starboard side of the battleship, away from the divers working below.

The patch, so close to being secured, could not be nudged any closer. Mud had been jetted and siphoned from beneath the turn of the bilge, down to the coral layer beneath. Divers chipped away at the tough coral with pneumatic mucking hammers and wedges, working in shifts of sixty to ninety minutes before being relieved.

A new challenge emerged when the leading edge of the bottom of the patch, having been maneuvered past the coral, hit the forward end of the wood-docking keel. The port and starboard keels, which took the weight of the hull when on blocks in drydock, now posed an obstacle. This section of the port keel had to be removed. Like the coral, the keel proved extraordinarily tough, and cutting it away was slow and difficult work.

On January 28, a new method was proposed: small charges of dynamite. A stick packed into a 6-inch length of hose was set off next to the keel, blowing a hole 10 inches deep and 6 inches wide. The following day, a hole was burned into the keel for a larger charge, which blew about 4 feet of keel several inches away from the hull. It was a promising start in overcoming this unexpected hurdle.

The unwatering of the ship progressed steadily, with minor leaks from drain and sanitary lines being plugged as they were discovered. A steel plate with a rubber mat was placed over the hole in the first platform deck made by the bomb that had exited near the keel, helping to limit the inflow of water to a trickle. The steel patch welded over the hole at the second deck had helped seal that one, but two others continued to leak, their location making it impossible to isolate them from the inside.

Ankers still hoped to remove enough water, stores, fuel, ammunition, and equipment to raise the draft to 32 feet and get *Nevada* into Dry Dock 1. To achieve this, the patches, particularly the large one, had to be secured as tight as possible to restrict the inevitable influx of water to an acceptable rate and permit the pumps to stay ahead of the flooding.

As the water receded, pumps were strategically placed to take suction on the next level down. The pumps not only had to draw water from below but had to lift it through discharge lines to pump it overboard. There was a constant balance between placing the pumps low in the ship to minimize the suction lift and keeping them as close to the top as possible to reduce the head of the discharge line.

By January 23, as divers labored to chip away the coral beneath the bilge, two 10-inch pumps had been placed on the second deck forward. With the exception of a few inches of water aft, the second deck was dry. Five days later, the pumping of the third deck commenced, and *Nevada*'s own fire and bilge pumps were rigged in the starboard engine room to drain the aft group of blisters. Lights and freshwater pipes were installed on the second deck as they had been on the main and upper decks, allowing working parties to remove trash and equipment and wash down the compartments.

Unwatering the ship, even at this slow rate while the patch was being fitted, was a delicate balancing act. The team had to decrease the draft of the battleship while maintaining equilibrium between the water pressure outside and inside the hull where it had been opened by the torpedo. The more water removed, the more buoyant the ship would become, improving the chances of docking her in Dry Dock 1. However, this meant pumping water from the spaces between frames 20 and 48, inboard of the damaged torpedo bulkheads and the patch.

The pressure difference between the water level outside the hull and that inside might collapse the patch as the ship was being towed across the channel to the yard. It was assumed that the patch had the strength to withstand a head of water of 10 feet—that is, a difference of 10 feet in the water levels on each side of it. Much less than that, and insufficient water would have been removed from the interior to obtain a satisfactory draft. Much more than that, and while the draft would decrease satisfactorily, the head of water would also increase, with a corresponding increase in water pressure exerted on the exterior of the patch.

To address these challenges, Holtzworth had devised a careful sixteen-step process of unwatering compartments, usually from fore to aft, deck by deck, excepting the area flooded between frames 20 and 48. His plan would ensure a safe head of water on the patch but, unless the strength of it had been dramatically underestimated, would not allow a docking in Dry Dock 1. The unwatering plan also considered the adhesion of the mud to the hull. Rather than try to overcome the suction of the mud along her entire length, the ship would be rocked gently up and down and peeled away from the bottom.

By February 3, *Nevada* had been unwatered down to the third deck, and the last of the docking keel had been dynamited off. Only minor trimming of wood scraps remained to be done. Two anchors had been set on the offshore side of the ship, in deeper

Nevada was grounded twice during her dash down the channel at Pearl Harbor: initially between the drydocks and Hospital Point, on the east side of the channel, and finally alongside Waipio Point, on the west side of the channel. This series of photos apparently was taken after the battleship was grounded off Waipio Point. On the opposite side of *Nevada*'s bow, harbor tug USS *Hoga* (YTM-146) is spraying water on the ship in an effort to quell the fires. The white shape on the hull along the waterline is a false wave that had been painted on, for camouflage and deception purposes. *A. D. Baker III collection*

USS *Hoga* (*foreground*), and the previously depicted USS *Avocet* are assisting *Nevada* after her beaching off Waipio Point. It was necessary to beach the ship because her anchor gear had been damaged during the bombing attack during the second wave of the Japanese attack. *National Archives*

Hoga and *Avocet* are seen from a different perspective in a photo directly facing the bow of the grounded *Nevada*. The battleship's starboard boat crane is swung out to the side. *National Archives*

The view of *Nevada* shifts slightly more to her starboard side as *Avocet* and *Hoga* continue to assist the ship. A steam of water is shooting from a hose aboard *Avocet*. *National Archives*

water, to hold her off the beach when she became waterborne. The diving teams began their last efforts to place the patch, free, it was assumed, from any further obstructions. Pumping continued, and calculations indicated that *Nevada* would float when the water level was 6 inches below the second platform deck.

On February 7, a tragic incident occurred that highlighted the dangers of the salvage operation. While testing for the presence of water in an adjacent compartment, Lt. Clarkson unscrewed an air test cap at a doorway and collapsed as water squirted out. Machinist's Mate First Class Peter Cornelius De Vries rushed to his aid and also collapsed, falling into the water. Four more men who rushed to help also collapsed almost immediately. De Vries and Clarkson later died, while the other four recovered after serious illness.

Initially thought to be carbon monoxide poisoning, further investigation revealed the culprit to be hydrogen sulfide gas. The gas, produced by the decomposition of organic materials under pressure, had been present throughout the unwatering process but was not thought to be hazardous. Under considerable water pressure, the gas was odorless and lethal. In some compartments, the concentration in the water itself could be as high as 300,000 parts per million.

In response to this tragedy, blowers and ventilation pipes were immediately run deep into *Nevada* to bring fresh air in and force contaminated air out. Despite this setback, the salvage operation continued with renewed caution.

As February progressed, *Nevada* continued to rise. By February 12 the vessel was rising about a foot a day. The watertight bulkheads beyond the patch were still holding as Ankers and his men carefully regulated the water being removed. At 1300 on February 13, Ankers officially reported his charge waterborne. *Nevada* was once again afloat, sixty-eight days after her valiant run for the sea ended on the shore of Hospital Point.

The ship was now scheduled for docking in Dry Dock 2 on February 18. The aircraft carrier *Saratoga* had left the dock for Bremerton after temporary repairs to her torpedo hit. Capt. Homer N. Wallin, in charge of Pearl Harbor's Salvage Division, had reported to Earle, the planning officer, that the gas hazard had greatly limited the amount of work that could be performed in lightening the ship, and efforts to reduce the draft sufficiently to get into Dry Dock 1 were discontinued.

As *Nevada*'s magazines were unwatered, 14-inch powder cans were unloaded to ammunition lighters for the trip to the

Nevada is viewed along her port beam, while considerable smoke is still issuing from her midsection, presumably after her final grounding off Waipio Point. All the 5-inch guns amidships are trained outward, and the several 3-inch antiaircraft guns are elevated in expectation of a renewed attack. *National Archives*

As smoke begins to clear from *Nevada,* the Measure 1/5 camouflage she is wearing is apparent. In addition to the previously seen false waves on the bow (now submerged), Measure 1/5 included Dark Gray (5-D) on vertical surfaces above the top of the smokestack, and Light Gray (L-5) on vertical surfaces above the smokestack. *National Archives*

Naval Ammunition Depot. On February 17, tugs ran lines to *Nevada*'s stern and towed her out to deeper water in the channel.

In a bold move, Ankers decided, with Wallin's concurrence, to remove the big patch altogether. This decision was not without risk—the patch, even though it couldn't be brought up tight against the hull, would still serve as a bulwark against water surging into the torpedo hole while the ship was towed across the channel entrance. The pressure could burst the inner bulkheads. However, divers had found the bottom of the patch extending nearly 4 feet below the keel, which would prohibit the docking of the ship regardless of which dock she headed for.

Throughout the night of February 17–18, pumps continued to drain the ship while a careful watch was kept on the bulkheads behind the torpedo damage. Fortunately, they continued to withstand the pressure head that Ankers and Mahan had so carefully maintained.

Early on the morning of February 18, the cables holding *Nevada* in position were slipped and secured to buoys for later recovery. Tugs came alongside and began the short push across the channel. The pumps were still going, keeping pace with the leaks. The ship drew just 31 feet aft but almost 42 feet forward, the result of the flooded forward compartments equalizing the pressure on the bulkheads open to the sea. Ballast tanks aft were flooded to bring her bow up, and she slid across the sill of Dry Dock 2 just before 1000.

As the dock emptied, water was pumped out of *Nevada*'s flooded bow to reduce her trim and the load on her keel as she settled bow first on the blocks. Adm. Nimitz was present to witness this milestone. He had looked glumly at her, blackened and flooded, when he first arrived at Pearl back in December. The commander in chief had taken a great interest in the progress of the salvage, and Wallin had briefed him weekly on the status of the work.

With *Nevada* now empty of water, a more accurate assessment of the damage was possible. Surprisingly, the ubiquitous presence of fuel oil, which had challenged the crew during the salvage operation, turned out to be a blessing in disguise. The oil had protected metal parts from corrosion while they were immersed in salt water. All the vital machinery, including the main engines, dynamos, and electrical motors, was salvageable—a tremendous factor in deciding the ship's future.

Navy Yard workers swiftly got to work. They replaced the temporary wooden patches on the hull with metal ones and rebuilt the affected portion of the antitorpedo blister. The starboard propeller and shaft, damaged during the second grounding, were fixed, as was the rudder. Inside, the gasoline tank and some other structures damaged by bombs were permanently mended, and machinery was disassembled, cleaned of oil, and put back into

With the fires aboard *Nevada* beginning to come under control, crewmen, many of whom are dressed in their skivvies, are starting to congregate on the decks. The national colors continue to wave from the flagstaff on the stern. Fires were a continuing concern after the ship's grounding off Waipio Point, with new fires often erupting as soon as others were extinguished. *National Archives*

Salvage work on *Nevada* and other ships at Pearl Harbor commenced soon after the December 7 attack. The battleship was grounded on a coral shelf and was stable. By the time this photo was taken, on December 9, engineers were assessing the prospects of salvaging the ship. Divers soon ascertained that no crewmen were trapped belowdecks.

operation. No attempt was made to deal with the wrecked superstructure beyond getting the galley functional. Top priority was to get *Nevada* out of Pearl Harbor and into a stateside yard for a thorough overhaul.

By April 3, 1942, Ens. C. W. Jenkins wrote in the war diary, "With a new coat of war paint on the exterior, the ship is now beginning to look like her old self." But the improvements were more than cosmetic: The next day, the ship was ready to feed her crew, and two days later, men began to come back on board for berthing.

On April 7, Adm. Nimitz visited *Nevada* to present medals for heroism demonstrated during the December 7 attack. In a brief speech on the quarterdeck, he said, "If a ship has personality and a soul, and I am convinced that she has, what a proud moment this must be for this gallant ship, whose sons are well represented in the list of honors about to be awarded." It was the first time since the attack that the officers and men of *Nevada* had appeared together in dress whites. Seven *Nevada* men received Navy Crosses, with six more Navy Crosses awarded after the ceremony, for a total of thirteen.

Eleven days later, on April 18, 1942, Adm. Nimitz, representing President Roosevelt, presented the Medal of Honor to Donald K. Ross. Ross had almost single-handedly kept *Nevada*'s dynamos running during the December 7 attack. Chief Boatswain Edwin Hill received the Medal of Honor posthumously for his crucial role in getting the ship underway on that fateful Sunday morning.

Nevada departed Pearl Harbor on April 22, 1942, bound for Puget Sound Navy Yard. She sailed in convoy with four merchant ships and six warships. As she steamed down the channel, *Nevada* cut an impressive figure, looking every bit the fighting ship. Her decks boasted three new scout planes, and all her guns were fully operational. While she still required extensive work, *Nevada* was combat ready.

The early days of the war saw resources stretched thin, prompting some in the Bureau of Ships (successor to the Bureau of Construction and Repair) to question the wisdom of investing heavily in a twenty-five-year-old battleship. Initial plans called for reconstructing *Nevada* to her December 6, 1941, configuration, with minor improvements such as remote control for her 5-inch/25-caliber antiaircraft battery and the addition of a sixteen-gun 20 mm battery.

However, the Chief of Naval Operations ultimately decided on a complete reconstruction of *Nevada*, effectively making her the prototype for renovating other Pearl Harbor survivors. The CNO ordered the mainmast replaced with a stump equipped with main and secondary battery directors, and the removal of boat cranes. To compensate for the planned increase in antiaircraft armament, weight reductions were necessary. Given the unlikelihood of *Nevada* engaging in traditional battleship duels, her heavily armored conning tower gave way to an open bridge and enclosed steering station, mirroring the Navy's latest cruiser designs.

Further weight savings came from reducing main battery ammunition to ninety rounds per gun, down thirty rounds per gun, saving 300 tons. This saved weight went into significantly upgrading *Nevada*'s secondary armament. Lessons from Pearl Harbor and expectations of airpower's growing influence in naval warfare led designers to equip *Nevada* with an extensive array of antiaircraft guns.

The ship's 5-inch/25-caliber batteries were replaced with eight mounts, each housing twin 5-inch/38-caliber guns. Additional air defenses included eight 40 mm quad gun mounts and forty 20 mm Oerlikon guns. Antiaircraft guns occupied nearly every available space on the deck and superstructure, an addition the crew would come to appreciate during future encounters with Japanese kamikaze attacks.

Nevada's silhouette changed dramatically, surprising her longtime crew members. The mainmast was shortened, and the smoke pipe canted aft to prevent smoke from obscuring the bridge. Turret 3 lost its catapult, leaving only the one on the quarterdeck; two planes were deemed sufficient for future scouting and spotting missions.

Equally significant as her new guns and aircraft was *Nevada*'s acquisition of cutting-edge radar equipment. This technology would allow for early detection of aircraft and surface vessels, significantly enhancing the ship's combat effectiveness.

Nevada's original design accommodated about one thousand men. However, the enhanced armament, improved fire control systems, and additional damage control personnel increased her wartime complement to over two thousand. This dramatic increase in crew size strained the ship's infrastructure, particularly in terms of berthing, food service, and fresh water supply.

On December 7, 1942, exactly one year after the Pearl Harbor attack, *Nevada* was underway, changing berths at Puget Sound. Her seven-and-a-half-month stay in the shipyard, costing $23 million, had transformed her into a modernized battleship ready to avenge Pearl Harbor.

An aerial photograph captured *Nevada* (*top of photo*) grounded alongside Waipio Point, with three support ships moored alongside her. At the lower right is Hospital Point, along which *Nevada* initially was grounded, on December 7, before being towed to Waipio Point. *Nevada*'s stern is pointing toward the top of the photo; the square object just off the stern is a barge with a large crane. *National Archives*

Another aerial photo, probably taken on the same occasion as the preceding one, shows the grounded *Nevada* from astern, with Waipio Point to the right, Hospital Point in the left background, and the entrance to the harbor in the right background. The crane barge is near the stern. *National Archives*

The blasts of the three bombs that punctured the upper deck, or forecastle deck, to the front of turret 1 caused the deck to buckle significantly, as seen in a photo taken on December 12, 1941. To the right is one of the small ships assisting *Nevada. National Archives*

Naval personnel are surveying the buckled deck below the guns of turret 1 on December 12. In the foreground is all that remains of an electric winch. The photo was taken from the minesweeper USS *Rail* (AM-26), which was moored along the starboard bow of *Nevada. Naval History and Heritage Command*

Damage to *Nevada*'s superstructure and upper works was extensive. This photo, taken on December 23, 1941, shows the devastation on the starboard side of the signal bridge. *National Archives*

Another December 23 view of the signal deck, taken from the captain's office, shows the port 3-pounder saluting gun at the center and a leg of the foremast toward the left. *National Archives*

Damage to the forecastle deck between frames 26 and 30 is seen, facing to starboard. Water is visible in the space below the deck. *National Archives*

A window-frame patch is being assembled in the shipfitters' shop at the Pearl Harbor Navy Yard in early January 1942. Once completed, it would be used to seal a bomb exit hole at the bottom of *Nevada*'s port bow until a permanent patch was installed. *Naval History and Heritage Command*

In order to temporarily close off the extensive torpedo damage on the port side of *Nevada*'s hull until the damage could be permanently repaired in drydock, this large patch was fabricated at the Pearl Harbor Navy Yard and was photographed in early January 1942. The patch was curved to fit under the turn of the bilge. *Naval History and Heritage Command*

The large patch for the breach in the hull from the torpedo has been hoisted, showing the interior of the assembly. The patch measured 55 by 32 feet. *Naval History and Heritage Command*

Turrets 1 and 2 and the foredeck of *Nevada* were photographed on January 15, 1942, while the battleship was still grounded off Waipio Point. The ruptured upper deck is visible to the front of turret 1. Salvage workers had already removed some of the buckled plating on the starboard side of the forecastle deck.

The Hawaiian Dredging Company crane barge *Gaylord* is transporting the large patch to *Nevada* at her grounded location off Waipio Point in January 1942. Attempts to achieve a watertight seal failed, due to bulging of the plates of the antitorpedo blister. Further, it was determined that the curved bottom would have interfered with drydocking the ship, so the patch was removed once *Nevada* was refloated. *Naval History and Heritage Command*

The salvage crew refloated *Nevada* on February 12, 1942. She was photographed on February 16 while she was being prepared for drydocking. Two days later, *Nevada* entered Dry Dock 2, where she would receive repairs sufficient to make her seaworthy for the voyage to the Puget Sound Navy Yard, where the ship would receive permanent repairs and undergo modernization. *Naval History and Heritage Command*

A photographer in the maintop of *Nevada* took this view of the foremast and foretop of *Nevada* while grounded off Waipio Point on February 16, 1942. At the bottom center is the top of the smokestack. The two turret-like structures between the smokestack and the foremast (the starboard one is easier to discern) are the Mk. 19 directors for the 5-inch guns. The A-frames mounted on the port side of the deck were temporary supports for chain falls, which, on the following day, would be assisting in lowering the temporary patch to cover the torpedo hole.

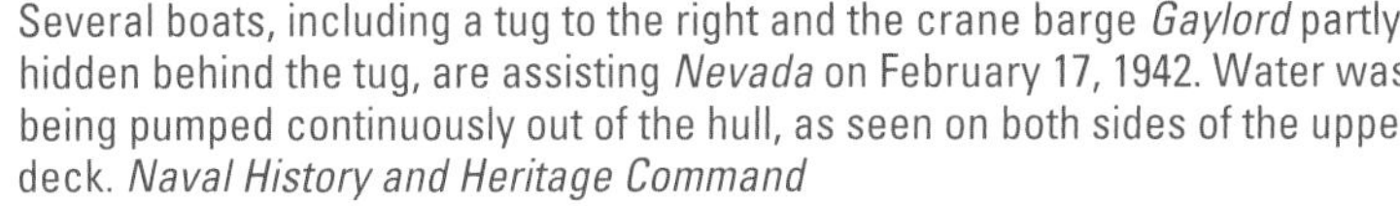

Several boats, including a tug to the right and the crane barge *Gaylord* partly hidden behind the tug, are assisting *Nevada* on February 17, 1942. Water was being pumped continuously out of the hull, as seen on both sides of the upper deck. *Naval History and Heritage Command*

On the same day the preceding photo was taken, February 17, the crane barge *Gaylord,* with the assistance of several tugs, removed the large temporary patch from the torpedo hole on the port side of *Nevada.* The crane has partially raised the patch in this photo; it had been determined that the battleship could make the trip across the harbor to the drydock without the patch. *Naval History and Heritage Command*

Riding low in the water but on a reasonably level keel on February 17, *Nevada* is being readied for drydocking on the following day. The buckled deck is visible to the front of turret 1. *Naval History and Heritage Command*

As seen in a bow-on photo of *Nevada*, under tow to Dry Dock 2 at the Pearl Harbor Navy Yard on February 18, 1942, the battleship had a slight but visible list to the starboard. *National Archives*

USS *Nevada* is being pulled into Dry Dock 2 at Pearl Harbor Navy Yard on February 18, 1942. The discoloration along the hull marks the waterline when the ship was beached. Many crewmen are on the decks, and it must have been a proud moment for them as their ship entered the drydock. *Naval History and Heritage Command*

Nevada has entered Dry Dock 2 at the Pearl Harbor Navy Yard on February 18, 1942, and the caisson, the huge gate that would close the harbor end of the drydock, is being closed.

On February 19, 1942, the day after *Nevada* entered drydock, the torpedo damage on the port side of the hull was photographed. The damage was roughly between frames 36 and 46. The blister plating was torn open. The flat plate inside the upper half of the opening is the lower part of the armor belt.

The breach in the hull from the torpedo is seen from a different perspective. Prior to drydocking, divers had cut away much of the torn plating of the blister. Toward the top of the photo is the armor shelf, at the top of the armor belt. *National Archives*

The man at the lower right provides a sense of the scale of the torpedo hole in the hull of *Nevada* in a photo taken on or around February 19, 1942. The belt armor is visible behind the upper part of the opening. *Naval History and Heritage Command*

The opening in the hull caused by the torpedo hit is observed from farther forward on February 20, 1942. According to the official damage report for USS *Nevada*, the torpedo exploded on contact with the blister, rather than after penetrating the blister. *National Archives*

The buckled upper deck below the three guns of turret 1 is observed facing to the port side. At the center is the starboard capstan. Damage-assessment personnel expressed surprise that the bomb blast fractured the wooden deck planks without much splintering. *National Archives*

Temporary repairs on USS *Nevada* were completed at Pearl Harbor in April 1942. On April 22, the battleship departed from Pearl Harbor under her own power, as seen here, bound for the Puget Sound Navy Yard (PSNY) in Bremerton, Washington, for more-permanent repairs and extensive modernization. Mounted on the catapults are three Vought OS2U Kingfisher observation planes. *National Archives*

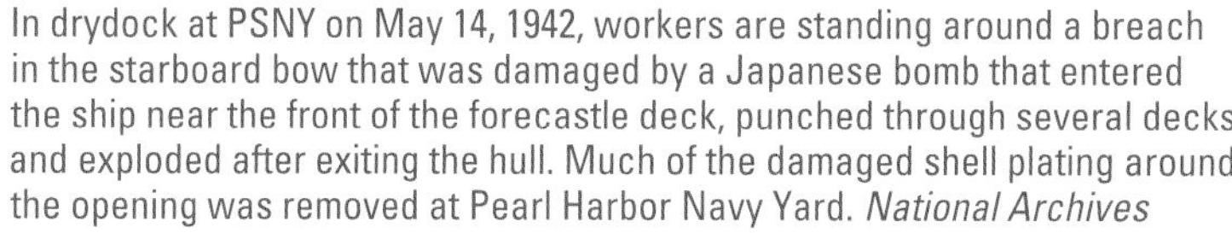

In drydock at PSNY on May 14, 1942, workers are standing around a breach in the starboard bow that was damaged by a Japanese bomb that entered the ship near the front of the forecastle deck, punched through several decks, and exploded after exiting the hull. Much of the damaged shell plating around the opening was removed at Pearl Harbor Navy Yard. *National Archives*

The same bomb damage is viewed facing aft. The workman is standing on the second platform; in Navy parlance, a platform is a partial deck below the lowest complete deck in the hull. To the right is bulkhead 14, which was in line with frame 14. *National Archives*

At PSNY on May 16, 1942, the area where the Japanese torpedo blew an opening in the blister on the port side of *Nevada*'s hull is shown. In the area where the white border has been marked on the photo, on the right side, starting at frame 40, is the lower part of a patch installed at Pearl Harbor Navy Yard. Workers at PSNY had enlarged the opening in the blister, spanning from frame 35 to frame 36, for more-permanent repairs. *National Archives*

In a photo taken on May 23, 1942, the area depicted in the preceding photo is at the bottom, above which, delineated by a white outline, is the upper part of a patch installed at Pearl Harbor Navy Yard. Toward the top of the photo is the ledge along the top of the blister. *National Archives*

***Nevada* General Data, 1942**	
Dimensions	
Length overall	583'0"
Waterline length	575'0"
Maximum beam	107'11"
Full-load draft	31'5 1⁄4"
Rebuilder	Puget Sound Naval Shipyard
Entered shipyard	January 2, 1928
Left shipyard	December 7, 1942
Displacement	
27,051 tons standard	
33,901 tons design emergency	
Armor Protection	
Belt	13.5" tapering to 8", 17'4 5⁄8" wide, 8'6" below water
Armor deck	80 lbs. STS + 50 lbs. STS + 50 lbs. STS + 20 lbs.; aft 180 lbs. STS + 70 lbs. amidships
Splinter deck	40 lbs. NS + 20 lbs. / 60 lbs. NS + 20 lbs. STS + 20 lbs. / 60 lbs. STS + 20 lbs.
Turrets	
Faceplates	18"; sides: 16"/5" STS / 10"–9"
Barbettes	
13" above second deck, 5" between second and half decks	
Armament	
Main battery	10 14"/.45
Secondary battery	16 5"/.38
AA battery	8 quad 40 mm Bofors + 40 single 20 mm Oerlikon
Machinery	
Boilers	6 Bureau Express 300 psi
Engines	2 geared turbines
Shaft horsepower	25,000 maximum ahead
Maximum speed	20.5 knots
Endurance	12 knots, 5,195 nautical miles
Rudders	1, balanced
Fuel	3,148 tons oil
Complement: 2,220	

In addition to repairing the battered hull of *Nevada*, Puget Sound Navy Yard also performed an extensive modernization of the ship, to ready her for the new realities of naval combat. In this photo from June 26, 1942, the guns have been removed from the ship; the old tripod mainmast has been moved forward, close behind the smokestack; the conning tower was removed and not replaced; and the old superstructure has been removed and replaced by a new one.

Nevada is seen from the starboard side at PSNY on June 26, 1942. Plans for the modernization of *Nevada* had been in the works months earlier, even as the battered battleship lay grounded in Pearl Harbor. Here, the roofs of all four turrets had been removed, and temporary peaked roofs were resting on top of the gunhouses.

CHAPTER 7

North to Alaska

Following her extensive rebuild, *Nevada* steamed to San Pedro, arriving on Christmas Day 1942. The ship's crew, largely inexperienced, required several months of rigorous training to achieve combat readiness. On April 7, 1943, *Nevada*, accompanied by *Idaho*, departed San Pedro. The two battleships set sail for Alaska on April 23, 1943, their mission shrouded in secrecy.

To maintain the covert nature of their operation, cold-weather gear was concealed, and the crew received briefings on tropical diseases. Officers were observed studying North Atlantic maps, further misdirecting attention from their true destination. *Nevada* formed part of Task Force (TF) 51, the assault force under RAdm. Francis W. Rockwell, tasked with executing Operation Landcrab—the mission to reclaim Attu Island from Japanese control.

On April 16, the task force dropped anchor in Kuluk Bay, Adak Island, situated approximately midway between Alaska's westernmost point and Japanese-held Attu. The following day, the task group ventured into enemy waters, a mere 400 miles from the Japanese naval stronghold at Paramushiro.

The ships pushed through harsh weather conditions, with *Nevada*'s 14-inch guns elevated to shield their muzzle bags from crashing waves. Despite the challenging environment, the crew's duties remained unrelenting. Destroyers required refueling, provisions needed transfer to smaller escorts, and constant vigilance was maintained. Weapons underwent cold-weather testing, and aircraft demanded meticulous maintenance to ensure flight readiness.

For those on deck, conditions were miserable. Snow squalls frequently reduced visibility to zero, while ice coated every surface. The peril of being washed overboard was ever present, with water temperatures at a frigid 28°F and air temperatures only marginally higher. A persistent fog hampered air operations and led to several collisions among the task force's smaller vessels. However, this same fog provided a natural shield against enemy aircraft, granting the Americans a tactical advantage.

Nevada's problematic steering mechanism once again proved troublesome. This issue was particularly concerning given the inaccuracy of available navigation charts. Capt. Kitts frequently ordered full reverse as the fathometer indicated rapidly diminishing water depths, sometimes as shallow as 10 fathoms. Visible rocky pinnacles hinted at treacherous underwater hazards capable of breaching the hull.

Nevada, along with *Pennsylvania* and *Idaho*, were assigned to provide naval gunfire support for the US Army Seventh Division's landing units. The battleships were joined by the escort carrier *Nassau*, tasked with close air support (CAS). These vessels, along with destroyers and additional support ships, formed the support group, Task Group (TG) 51.1. On May 1, the task force assembled at Cold Bay. Four days later, TG 51.1, now comprising three battleships and twenty-four support vessels, departed. They navigated along the Aleutians' southern coast and entered the Bering Sea via Amutka Pass to evade detection.

The invasion of Attu commenced on May 11 at Holtz Bay, on the island's northeastern sector. While *Pennsylvania*, *Idaho*, and their escorts provided fire support and weathered at least two torpedo attacks from Japanese submarines, *Nevada*, serving as Admiral Rockwell's flagship, was tasked with supporting the invasion at Massacre Bay on the island's southern portion. She provided heavy firepower for the largest concentration of invasion troops, carried by three transports.

On May 12 at 0715, General Quarters sounded aboard *Nevada*. Thirty-one minutes later, her main battery opened fire on Japanese shore positions. Two spotter planes were launched to guide the fall of shells. Despite fog delaying the landing and causing anxiety among the Army personnel, the invasion proceeded by midday.

The landing proved challenging, with rough seas capsizing one landing craft and forcing another onto the rocks. *Nevada*'s supporting fire proved crucial in securing the beachhead, since the invasion at Massacre Bay occurred in full view of Japanese positions. Her main and secondary batteries unleashed a barrage on the ridges above the bay, where Japanese forces had retreated prior to the invasion.

Despite the Japanese being well dug in, the high-explosive shells took their toll. Despite the bombardment, the Japanese managed to rain shells down on the American positions, rendering the supposedly secure beachhead anything but safe. Throughout the day, *Nevada*'s 14-inch battery engaged targets on four separate occasions due to the intermittent nature of the action.

On May 13, Adm. Rockwell ordered *Nevada* to move closer inshore, aiming to minimize response time to fire support requests. Over the next three days, the battleships unleashed a tremendous barrage, nearly depleting their ammunition stores. On May 14, they set course for Adak to replenish their magazines.

Modernization of *Nevada* at PSNY was completed in early December 1942, and on December 9 she began gunnery tests. She is seen here and in the following photos during sea trials off Restoration Point, Puget Sound, Washington, on December 14. Among the new features on the ship are the raked extension smokestack (designed to keep the bridges clear of smoke), the shortened and relocated mainmast, and the twin 5-inch/38-caliber dual-purpose gun mounts amidships, four on each side. The catapult had been removed from turret 3, leaving a single catapult on the fantail. *National Archives*

New Mexico and *Mississippi*, two battleships transferred from the Atlantic to the Pacific by CNO Stark following the Pearl Harbor attack, joined the formation on May 22. By this time, the remaining 2,630 Japanese defenders on Attu faced a dire situation, with dwindling numbers and scarce supplies. In a desperate gambit, one thousand Japanese troops launched a banzai charge against American lines, initially aiming to capture US artillery and supplies rather than as a suicide attack.

Brig. Gen. Archibald Arnold rallied his troops and directed their fire onto the charging Japanese. By day's end, US forces had eliminated half of the attackers, with the remainder taking their own lives. A smaller charge the following day met the same fate, marking the end of the battle for Attu.

The Attu campaign, despite its small scale, ranked among the Pacific theater's bloodiest battles. The Japanese defenders were almost entirely annihilated, while US casualties exceeded the original number of Japanese troops on the island by 50 percent. For *Nevada*, it marked the first of many instances where her commanding officer would disregard potential danger to provide close bombardment support.

Capt. Kitts received the Legion of Merit for his role in the Attu campaign, a testament to his leadership and the ship's performance under challenging conditions.

The subsequent operation to reclaim Kiska initially appeared to follow a similar pattern. Relentless bombing by Army aircraft was followed by bombardment from *New Mexico* and *Mississippi*. However, these efforts proved futile. On July 28, Japanese cruisers and destroyers executed a daring mission to the island, successfully evacuating over five thousand troops. When 34,000 American forces landed, they found Kiska deserted.

As seen during sea trials in Puget Sound, the modernized *Nevada* had much more substantial upper works than before modernization. Part of the extra weight imposed by the new superstructure, directors, and other structures was compensated by the removal of the thickly armored conning tower and the boat cranes, the shortening of the mainmast, and the reduction in size and mass of the fighting tops. *A. D. Baker III collection*

Eight quadruple 40 mm gun mounts and forty-one single 20 mm gun mounts were installed on *Nevada* during her 1942 modernization. As seen from above her starboard quarter, single 20 mm gun mounts inside D-shaped splinter shields are on each side of the catapult, while a quadruple 40 mm gun mount is inside a circular splinter shield to the side of turret 3. More 40 mm and 20 mm gun mounts are located on the superstructure. *National Archives*

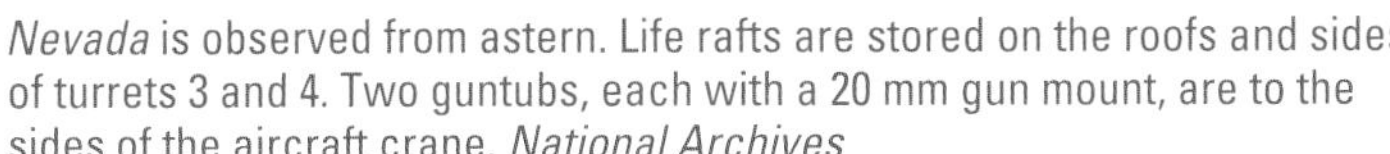

Nevada is observed from astern. Life rafts are stored on the roofs and sides of turrets 3 and 4. Two guntubs, each with a 20 mm gun mount, are to the sides of the aircraft crane. *National Archives*

As seen in a view off *Nevada*'s port stern, the ship's number, 36, was now painted on the side of the stern; it also was painted on both sides of the bow, aft of the anchors. Air-search and surface-search radars had been installed during the modernization. The tops of the foremast and the shortened mainmast retained the old Mk. 20 directors, but they now were in cylindrical housings. Four new Mk. 37 secondary-battery directors replaced the old directors on the masts; three were mounted on the superstructure: one forward and one on each side. A fourth Mk. 37 director was atop the deckhouse just aft of the stub mainmast. *National Archives*

In a view of *Nevada* at PSNY on December 15, 1942, on the forecastle are two single 20 mm gun mounts, located in tandem inside a splinter shield. Three of the four new Mk. 37 directors are in view: the forward one, above the navigating bridge; the portside director, adjacent to the smokestack; and the aft Mk. 37, aft of the stub mainmast. Each Mk. 37 director has a Mk. 4 fire-control radar antenna mounted above it. Mounted above the main-battery directors atop the two masts are Mk. 3 fire-control radar antennas, and an SC-1 air-search radar antenna is faintly visible on top of the aft main-battery director. *Randy Fagan, The Floating Drydock collection*

A barge is to the left in a December 15, 1942, view of *Nevada* at PSNY. The white number 36 on the bow was painted on a round steel plate welded over where the spare-anchor hawsehole formerly was located, that anchor having been eliminated during the recent modernization. New features on the superstructure included an enclosed pilothouse and an open navigating bridge. *Randy Fagan, The Floating Drydock collection*

The barge remains in place in this view off the port bow of *Nevada* on December 15, 1942. Partway up the foremast is a platform with two 36-inch searchlights. Above the main-battery director atop the foremast are, *front*, the director radar antenna, and *rear*, a parabolic surface-search radar antenna. *Randy Fagan, The Floating Drydock collection*

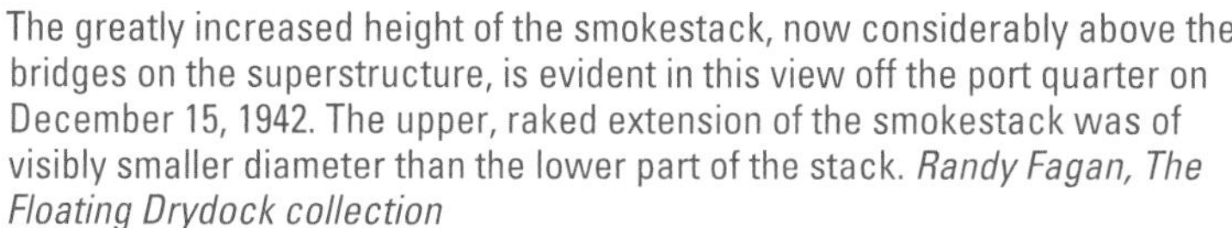

The greatly increased height of the smokestack, now considerably above the bridges on the superstructure, is evident in this view off the port quarter on December 15, 1942. The upper, raked extension of the smokestack was of visibly smaller diameter than the lower part of the stack. *Randy Fagan, The Floating Drydock collection*

Nevada is seen from astern at PSNY on December 15, 1942. A clear view is available of the semiconical sponsons below the tubs for the 20 mm guns on the stern. The rear terminus of the blister on each side of the hull is visible. *National Archives*

From April to June 1943, USS *Nevada* served a deployment in the Aleutian Islands, operating against Japanese forces that had invaded the islands of Attu and Kiska the previous year. During *Nevada*'s service in Alaskan waters, a photographer snapped this photo from the port side of the ice- and snow-covered main deck, facing toward the stern. In addition to the 20 mm guntub on the stern next to the aircraft crane, there are three more 20 mm gun galleries inside splinter shields in view; the guns have been dismounted and the cradles protected with fabric covers. Parts of two motorboats are seen to the far left. *National Archives*

USS *Nevada* is underway in the vicinity of Attu on a foggy day during May 1943. The two OS2U Kingfisher observation planes mounted in tandem on the catapult feature large national insignia on the fuselages: a white star inside a blue circle. On their vertical tails are prominent vertical white stripes. *National Archives*

CHAPTER 8

Return to the Atlantic

Following her service in the Aleutian campaign, *Nevada* steamed into San Francisco in June 1943 for a brief maintenance period at Mare Island Navy Yard, Vallejo, California. On July 1, 1943, the battleship embarked on a southward journey to Panama. After navigating the Panama Canal, she set course for the Norfolk Navy Yard, where she would undergo further modernization in preparation for her new role in supporting amphibious landings in the European Theater of Operations.

Upon completion of her yard period, *Nevada* shifted to Boston before anchoring in Gravesend Bay, New York, on September 2, 1943. The following day, she departed as part of convoy UT-2, tasked with escorting cargo vessels to the United Kingdom. On September 14, 1943, *Nevada* dropped anchor in Belfast Lough, Ireland, having successfully delivered her charges. Shortly thereafter, she escorted the return convoy, TU-2, back to American shores before proceeding to Boston Navy Yard for much-needed maintenance.

The ensuing months saw *Nevada* return to convoy duty, her itinerary including stops in New York, Maine, Massachusetts, and Ireland. This routine was punctuated by another visit to Boston Navy Yard, after which she steamed to Casco Bay, Maine, on March 21, 1944, for engine trials and gunnery training. On March 29, the focus shifted to bombardment practice, with *Nevada* unleashing her formidable guns on Seal Island, situated 21 miles off Rockland, Maine.

Upon her return to Boston, *Nevada* underwent a significant change to her armament. The ship's magazines were reconfigured, with 514 14-inch armor-piercing rounds being removed and replaced by 578 high-capacity (high explosive) rounds. This modification reflected the changing nature of her mission, as *Nevada* prepared for her role in the upcoming invasion of Europe.

After one final day of bombardment practice, *Nevada*, accompanied by *Arkansas*, set sail from Casco Bay on April 18, 1944. Their destination was British waters, where they would prepare for Operation Neptune, the naval component of Operation Overlord—the long-awaited invasion of Normandy.

As D-Day approached, *Nevada* was assigned to TF 125's bombardment group under RAdm. Morton L. Deyo. Her mission was to provide fire support for the Allied landings on Utah Beach. The battleship found herself in distinguished company, joined by the heavy cruisers *Tuscaloosa* and *Quincy*, the British heavy cruiser *Hawkins*, light cruisers *Enterprise* and *Black Prince*, the monitor *Erebus*, and the Dutch gunboat *Soemba*. This formidable fleet took up positions between the vulnerable transports and the German batteries ashore, ready to unleash their combined firepower.

On June 6, 1944, at 0536, *Nevada* opened fire, her guns roaring to life fourteen minutes ahead of schedule in response to incoming fire from German batteries. For the next fifty minutes, extending beyond H-hour, the task force hammered the German defenses. *Nevada*'s primary target was a German gun emplacement at Azeville, just north of the Utah landing site. As the invasion progressed, she shifted her fire to engage German positions near St. Vaast-la-Hogue before providing close support to US 101st Airborne Division units battling to secure Sainte-Mère-Église and the vital causeways linking the beaches to the main Allied axis of advance toward Cherbourg.

The following day, June 7, saw *Nevada* engage fourteen different targets. In one notable action, she unleashed forty-three 14-inch rounds to break up a German concentration north of the US Fourth Infantry Division. On June 8, between 0557 and 0940, she targeted five casemated batteries and strongpoints. Later that morning, at 1023, *Nevada* fired seventy 14-inch rounds at a concentration of an estimated 110 German tanks and other vehicles, located 23,500 yards away. Her spotter aircraft reported total destruction or damage of all vehicles in the target area.

Following this intense period of action, *Nevada* retired to Plymouth, England, for replenishment. Her contribution to the invasion had been substantial, having fired 926 14-inch and 3,491 5-inch rounds in support of the landing forces. After resupply, she returned to the Utah Beach gunline, continuing to provide naval gunfire support until June 13, when she was reassigned to the Omaha Beach area. *Nevada* finally withdrew from the Normandy action on June 17, 1944.

The battleship's respite was short-lived. On June 22, 1944, *Nevada* rendezvoused with Rear Admiral Deyo's Task Force (TF) 129, the Cherbourg Bombardment force, assembling at Portland, England. At 0430 on June 25, she departed Portland as part of Group One, sailing in company with *Tuscaloosa*, *Quincy*, *Enterprise*, the light cruiser *Glasgow*, and a screening force of five destroyers. This group was complemented by Group Two, comprising *Texas*, *Arkansas*, and their own destroyer screen.

At 1030, *Nevada* and her group moved into Fire Support Area 1, approximately 28,000 yards north of Cherbourg. By noon, they had closed to within 12,000 yards of the shore. As the ships awaited fire support requests from advancing US Army units,

German shore batteries opened fire at 1206. The ensuing engagement was intense, with German gunners demonstrating remarkable accuracy. *Nevada* found herself bracketed by a three-gun salvo, one shell landing within 100 yards of the ship.

Between 1240 and 1245, German guns bracketed *Nevada* six times. However, Capt. Powell M. Rhea's skillful maneuvering kept the battleship from sustaining any direct hits. As some task force ships took damage, the accompanying destroyers laid smoke to obscure the targets. Despite these challenging conditions, Group One successfully bombarded and silenced the battery at Querqueville.

Throughout the action, *Nevada* responded to numerous calls for fire from shore-based fire control parties. At 1212, she engaged a target approximately 2.5 miles southwest of Querqueville with her 14-inch battery. By 1229, her shells were finding their mark, and within five minutes, *Nevada* had delivered eighteen 14-inch rounds. After twenty-five minutes of sustained bombardment, the Germans displayed a white panel at 1237, signaling their surrender.

Using her spotting aircraft, *Nevada* then shifted fire to new targets between Querqueville and La Rivière. She continued to engage targets of opportunity until ceasing fire at 1525. In total, *Nevada* had expended 112 14-inch and 985 5-inch rounds during the engagement. Despite being straddled by enemy fire more than twenty times, the battleship emerged with only superficial damage from shell fragments and, remarkably, no casualties.

This impressive performance at Cherbourg earned *Nevada* the nickname "Old Imperishable." With Allied armies advancing into the French interior, she withdrew to Londonderry, Northern Ireland, for a well-deserved period of rest and replenishment.

On July 4, 1944, *Nevada* set sail for the Mediterranean Sea. After transiting the Straits of Gibraltar, she arrived at Oran, Algeria, where her crew learned of their next mission: Operation Dragoon, the invasion of southern France. For this operation, *Nevada* joined a formidable task force including *Texas*; the light cruiser *Philadelphia*; French light cruisers *Montcalm* and *Georges Leygues*; and large destroyers *Le Fantasque*, *Le Terrible*, and *Le Malin*; along with seven additional destroyers. This group, designated TF 85 gunfire support group under RAdm. Carleton F. Bryant, was assigned to support the Delta landing sites near the Golfe de St. Tropez.

The initial landings on August 15, 1944, encountered minimal resistance. However, the situation intensified on August 19, when *Nevada*, alongside the French battleship *Lorraine* and heavy cruiser *Augusta*, conducted a reconnaissance in force off Toulon. Their mission was to support the US Army's Third Division and French troops advancing on the port. Escorted by four destroyers, the group engaged harbor defenses and 13.4-inch-gun batteries at St. Mandrier, these guns having been salvaged from French battleships scuttled earlier in the war.

In a notable engagement, *Nevada* traded fire with the German-manned French battleship *Strasbourg*, scoring hits that caused

After departing from Alaskan waters, the battleship proceeded to San Francisco, where she underwent repairs and reprovisioning. *Nevada* is seen here departing from San Francisco on July 1, 1943. Two Vought OS2U Kingfisher observation planes are present: one on the catapult, and one on the deck. Above the aft main-battery director, halfway up the air-search radar mast is a recently installed surface-search radar, to supplement the similar set above the foretop. *National Archives*

While underway in San Francisco Bay on July 1, 1943, a photographer in an aircraft from Naval Air Station Alameda, California, snapped this view from 800 feet above *Nevada*'s bow. The splinter shield for the two tandem 20 mm gun mounts on the forecastle had a curved front and was open at the rear for entrance and egress of the crewmen. Six 20 mm ammunition lockers are on the inner sides of the splinter shield. The dark areas on the turret roofs were floating nets: large nets with flotation devices attached, which would be thrown overboard for the crew to cling to in the event the ship was sunk. *National Archives*

Also taken from an altitude of 800 feet on July 1, 1943, is a view of *Nevada* from over her stern. Assembled on the decks are large and small groups of crewmen wearing dress blues and white caps. The national insignia on the two Kingfisher observation planes are the recently introduced type, with white bars on the sides and a red border. *National Archives*

the enemy vessel to list to starboard. Despite losing her spotter plane to German fire, *Nevada* continued her bombardment, successfully targeting all fortified gun emplacements before withdrawing under the cover of smoke laid by a screening destroyer.

Returning the following day, *Nevada* reengaged and neutralized the repaired German guns at Cape Sicie. On August 24, she received orders to proceed toward Marseilles to engage shore batteries on the islands of d'If, Pomeques, and Ratonneau, which had been harassing US supply ships entering the recently liberated port. After making corrections to compensate for her worn gun barrels, *Nevada* destroyed three batteries, disabled a fourth, and partially neutralized a fifth. Her final action involved destroying an enemy turret overlooking the harbor entrance.

With her mission in the Mediterranean complete, *Nevada* received orders to withdraw and proceed to Norfolk via Algiers for refit in preparation for deployment to the Pacific. En route, she was diverted to New York on September 13, arriving the next day. After a brief visit, the battleship departed for Norfolk on September 17, reaching her destination the following day.

At Norfolk Navy Yard, *Nevada* underwent a comprehensive overhaul, including the relining of her gun barrels and completely replacing the weapons in turret 1 with guns salvaged from turret 2 of USS *Arizona*. Upon completion of the work, she conducted trials on November 6–7, 1944. On November 21 the rejuvenated battleship steamed for the Panama Canal, ready to take the fight back to the Japanese home islands.

Another July 1, 1943, photo of *Nevada* was taken from an altitude of 900 feet as she proceeded in San Francisco Bay. Life rafts are on the sides of the turrets, and a paravane is stored on the side of turret 2. *National Archives*

This final photo of USS *Nevada* off San Francisco on July 1, 1943, was taken from an altitude of 800 feet. In addition to the platform partway up the foremast for two 36-inch searchlights, there was a platform for two 36-inch searchlights on the stub mainmast, below the aft main battery director. *National Archives*

USS *Nevada* is underway at sea on July 14, 1943. By this time, the ship was painted in Measure 21 camouflage, consisting of Navy Blue (5-N) on all vertical surfaces and Deck Blue (20-B) on all horizontal surfaces. *A. D. Baker III collection*

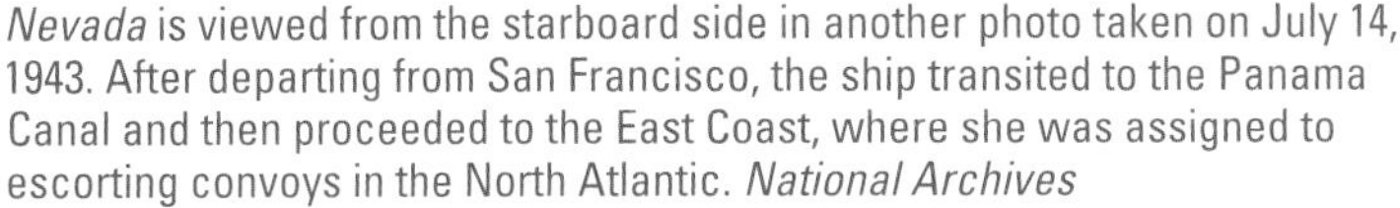

Nevada is viewed from the starboard side in another photo taken on July 14, 1943. After departing from San Francisco, the ship transited to the Panama Canal and then proceeded to the East Coast, where she was assigned to escorting convoys in the North Atlantic. *National Archives*

A photographer in an aircraft based at Naval Air Station Coco Solo, in the Canal Zone, took these July 14, 1943, aerial photos of *Nevada*. As built, there were three wildcats (i.e., the anchor capstans) on the foredeck, but the one on the starboard side of the deck was eliminated when the spare anchor on the port side was deleted. The two remaining wildcats are below the 14-inch gun tubes of turret 1. *National Archives*

On July 14, 1943, *Nevada* is observed from above her bow, offering a slightly different perspective from the preceding photograph. A light-colored cover is rigged over the canopy of the OS2U Kingfisher spotted on the deck next to the catapult.
National Archives

Following the transit from San Francisco to the Panama Canal, USS *Nevada* proceeded to Norfolk Navy Yard, Virginia, where she was prepared for convoy duty in the North Atlantic. The ship was repainted in Measure 22 camouflage, as seen in this August 23, 1943, photograph. This camouflage scheme consisted of Navy Blue (5-N) from the boot topping to the lowest point of the main deck, and from that level up, Haze Gray (5-H) on vertical surfaces. All horizontal surfaces were painted Deck Blue (20-B). A visible new change to the superstructure was the addition of bulwarks to the sides of the cylindrical foundation of the forward Mk. 37 director, at the top of the superstructure. *National Archives*

This starboard view of *Nevada* was taken at Norfolk Navy Yard on August 23, 1943. While at Norfolk, an SK "bed-spring" radar antenna was installed above the foretop, and, in order to clear the SK antenna, the surface-search radar antenna was placed on a topmast to the rear of the SK antenna. The 14-inch gun tubes were painted Deck Blue on their tops and Haze Gray on the sides and bottoms. *National Archives*

Further details of the new SK radar antenna above the foretop are evident in this view of *Nevada* off her starboard quarter at Norfolk Navy Yard, on August 23, 1943. Observation planes assigned to battleships and cruisers would fly to bases ashore when the ships went into navy yards for extensive work, and the ships would reembark the aircraft upon departing for sea. *National Archives*

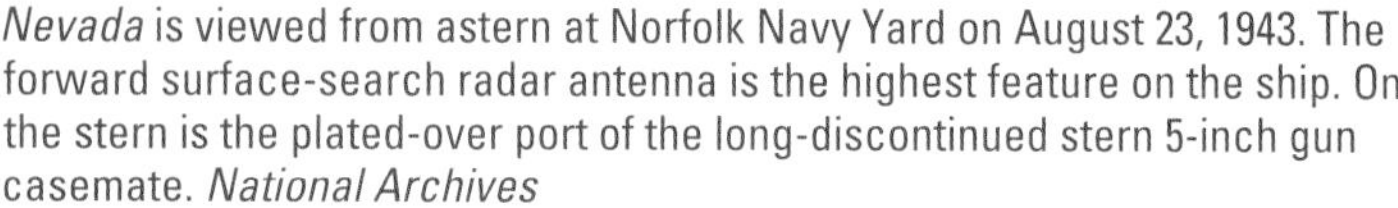
Nevada is viewed from astern at Norfolk Navy Yard on August 23, 1943. The forward surface-search radar antenna is the highest feature on the ship. On the stern is the plated-over port of the long-discontinued stern 5-inch gun casemate. *National Archives*

Accompanied by a tugboat, *Nevada* is observed head on at Norfolk Navy Yard on August 23, 1943. Jutting from both sides of the upper, or forecastle, deck are leadman's platforms; a crewman is standing on the starboard one. These portable platforms were emplaced as seen here when the ship was navigating in harbors or shallow channels. The leadman would drop a lead line (one is dangling from each platform) into the water to gauge the depth and would shout out the results to personnel on the bridge. In the left background is the downtown Norfolk waterfront. *National Archives*

Following gunnery practice in Chesapeake Bay in late August 1943, *Nevada* departed for the Atlantic on September 2, 1943, bound for New York City to commence convoy-escort operations. The ship is seen here on that date, underway at sea. Details of her new Measure 22 camouflage are shown to good advantage.

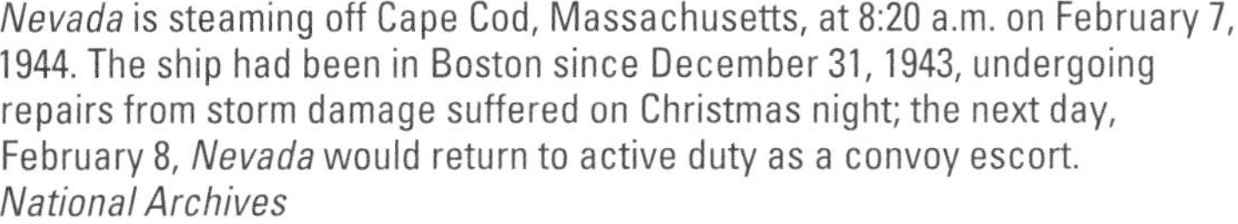

Nevada is steaming off Cape Cod, Massachusetts, at 8:20 a.m. on February 7, 1944. The ship had been in Boston since December 31, 1943, undergoing repairs from storm damage suffered on Christmas night; the next day, February 8, *Nevada* would return to active duty as a convoy escort. *National Archives*

In the spring of 1944, *Nevada*, as part of Battleship Division 5, prepared for participation in support of the D-Day invasion of Normandy. The ship is in the foreground, in Belfast Lough, Northern Ireland, on May 14, 1944, with USS *Texas* (BB-35) to the right. During this period, Battleship Division 5 was engaged in tactical maneuvers, firing practice for the main and the secondary batteries, and rehearsals for shore bombardments. *National Archives*

Crewmen are sweeping the main deck of *Nevada* on May 30, 1944, during preparations for the D-Day invasion. Turrets 3 and 4 are in the foreground. Worthy of notice is the difference in designs of the rangefinder objectives, protruding from the upper rear corners of the sides of the turrets. *National Archives*

Members of *Nevada*'s crew have gathered on the fantail to listen to an orchestra concert on May 30, 1944. Fabric muzzle covers are fitted over the 14-inch/45-caliber guns of turrets 3 and 4. Blast bags are present on the 14-inch/45-caliber guns as well as the 5-inch/38-caliber dual-purpose guns. They were termed "dual purpose" because they were equally effective against aircraft and surface targets. *National Archives*

Sailors and members of the US Marine contingent who are enjoying the orchestra concert on May 30 were photographed from the port guntub on the stern of *Nevada*. The rough-textured material on the roof of turret 4 is a floating net. *National Archives*

An officer on the fantail of *Nevada* is reading to crewmen instructions from Adm. Alan G. Kirk, senior US Navy commander in the invasion of Normandy, on June 2, 1944, four days before the D-Day landings. The instructions included information on where and when the landings would take place. *National Archives*

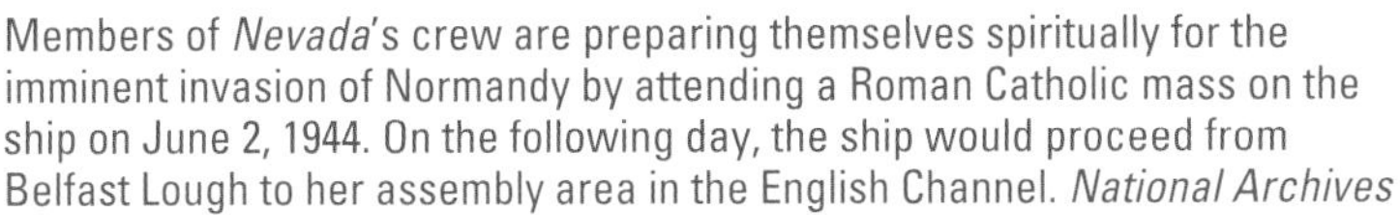

Members of *Nevada*'s crew are preparing themselves spiritually for the imminent invasion of Normandy by attending a Roman Catholic mass on the ship on June 2, 1944. On the following day, the ship would proceed from Belfast Lough to her assembly area in the English Channel. *National Archives*

The 14-inch/45-caliber guns of turrets 1 and 2 are trained to port, ready to bombard German defenses on an invasion beach in Normandy on June 6, 1944. At the lower right, a crewman is at work in a lookout station. *National Archives*

In a photograph taken from the cruiser USS *Quincy* (CA-71), turret 3 of USS *Nevada* has just loosed a salvo at German positions in support of US troops landing at Utah Beach on June 6, 1944. *Nevada* is still painted in Measure 22 camouflage. *National Archives*

The 14-inch/45-caliber guns of turrets 1 and 2 of *Nevada* have just fired a salvo at German defenses in support of the landings on Utah Beach on D-Day. *Nevada* began her bombardment at 5:47 a.m., first striking at German targets inland with her 14-inch guns and at targets near the shore with her secondary battery. *Nevada* fired a total of 337 14-inch rounds on D-Day. *National Archives*

Two of *Nevada*'s twin 5-inch/38-caliber gun mounts were photographed during a pause in the firing on D-Day. Spent 5-inch cartridge cases litter the deck below and heat has blistered off the paint in multiple areas on the 5-inch barrels. *Nevada*'s 5-inch/38-caliber guns fired a total of 2,693 rounds on D-Day. On racks on the inside of the circular splinter shield of the quadruple 40 mm gun mount are scores of clips of 40 mm ready ammunition. *National Archives*

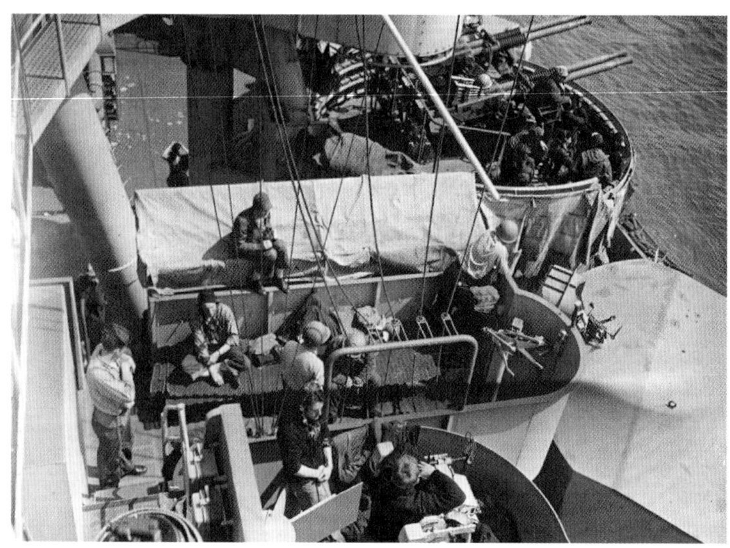

In a photograph taken from the port side of *Nevada*'s navigating bridge on D-plus-1, June 7, 1944, crewmen relax during a pause in the action. At the bottom center is a Mk. 51 director, for controlling the fire of 40 mm batteries. At the center, covered by a tarpaulin, is the port flag bag. At the bottom right is the top of a twin 5-inch/38-caliber gun mount, just beyond which is a quadruple 40 mm gun mount. *National Archives*

Three *Nevada* crewmen are standing watch on the starboard signal bridge as other crewmen nap during a lull in the action off Normandy on June 7, 1944. The flag bags, also called flag boards or flag lockers, housed the ship's signal flags. *National Archives*

After lending fire support to the Allied invasion force in Normandy on D-Day, June 6, 1944, and the ensuing days, USS *Nevada* repaired to Belfast Lough for a few days before being dispatched to the Mediterranean to lend firepower to Operation Dragoon, the Allied invasion of southern France. A photographer on the light cruiser USS *Philadelphia* (CL-41) took this undated photo of USS *Nevada* (*center*) and other ships of the fleet as they steamed to the invasion beaches. The journey from *Nevada*'s anchorage at Belfast Lough to the invasion beaches lasted from July 4 to August 15, with several stops for training and reprovisioning en route. *National Archives*

Following her service in the invasion of southern France, USS *Nevada* is nearing the East Coast of the United States on September 17, 1944. Her heavily weathered surfaces are still bearing the Measure 22 camouflage, but that would soon change. Two Vought Kingfishers are spotted in tandem on the catapult. *A. D. Baker III collection*

Nevada reported to Norfolk Navy Yard, Virginia, on September 18, 1944, and underwent an overhaul lasting almost two months. Among other improvements, turret 1 was rearmed with 14-inch/45-caliber guns salvaged from turret 2 of USS *Arizona* (BB-39) after her sinking. Also, as seen in a photo taken on November 8, 1944, at Norfolk, the ship was repainted in Camouflage Measure 31a, Design 6B, which featured patterns of three colors, Haze Gray (5-H), Ocean Gray (5-O), and Navy Blue (5-N), on the vertical surfaces and Deck Blue (20-B) on decks and horizontal surfaces. The following sequence of photos also was taken off Norfolk Navy Yard on November 8, 1944. *Randy Fagan, The Floating Drydock collection*

Nevada was riding high in the water when these photos were taken on November 8; the bottom of the black boot topping, normally submerged when the ship was fully loaded, is visible above the surface of the water. The lightest shade of paint is Haze Gray; Ocean Gray is the intermediate shade, and Navy Blue is the darkest. *Randy Fagan, The Floating Drydock collection*

The scheme for the Camouflage Measure 31a, Design 6B, as applied to USS *Nevada* in late 1944 at Norfolk Navy Yard is documented in this US Navy Bureau of Ships diagram dated October 14, 1944. *National Archives*

Nevada presents her port side off Norfolk Navy Yard. A small but important detail, visible here only under high magnification, is the addition of combination Mk. 12/ Mk. 22 fire-control radar antennas above each of the Mk. 37 secondary-battery directors. These replaced the original Mk. 4 antennas installed in 1942. The Mk. 22 antenna, mounted on the right side of the much-larger Mk. 12 antenna, was nicknamed "orange peel" because of its curved shape. The Mk. 22 added the ability of tracking low-flying aircraft to the Mk. 12's capabilities. *Randy Fagan, The Floating Drydock collection*

A new modification visible in this view from astern was the cut-down sides of the 20 mm guntubs on the stern; previously, the tops of the tubs were of the same height around their circumference. *Randy Fagan, The Floating Drydock collection*

Nevada is backlit in this view, with the Norfolk waterfront in the left background. Above the maintop are the SK air-search radar antenna, above which is the forward SG surface-search radar antenna. *Randy Fagan, The Floating Drydock collection*

The State of Nevada wanted to do something for the men aboard the battleship bearing the name of their state; thus, Governor E. P. Carville had sent this chest, containing a silver dollar—mined in Nevada—for each man aboard the ship. On November 19, 1944, Capt. Homer Grosskopf, who'd relieved Capt. Rhea on October 4, presented the coins to the crew. *National Archives*

CHAPTER 9

Once More to the Pacific

On December 10, 1944, *Nevada* arrived at Long Beach, California, where she spent the following weeks engaged in extensive gunnery and communications drills. The battleship's crew worked tirelessly to take on ammunition and supplies, preparing for their next deployment. Christmas 1944 found *Nevada* at anchor in Long Beach, a brief respite before her return to the Pacific theater.

On December 28, 1944, *Nevada* departed as part of Task Group (TG) 52.11, bound for the western Pacific. After a monthlong journey across the vast ocean, the task group rendezvoused with the fleet at Ulithi in the Caroline Islands on January 23, 1945. Four days later, on January 27, RAdm. Bertram J. Rodgers embarked *Nevada*, breaking his flag as commander of the Gunfire and Covering Force (TF 54).

Nevada set sail from Ulithi on February 10, 1945, as a unit of TG 54.9.2. She was in distinguished company, sailing alongside *Idaho*, *Tennessee*, the heavy cruisers *Chester* and *Pensacola*, and ten escort vessels. Two days later, on February 12, the task group arrived off Tinian to participate in rehearsals for the impending assault on Iwo Jima in the Bonin Islands.

With rehearsals complete, Task Force (TF) 54—now a formidable assemblage including the command ship *Estes*, *Nevada*, and five additional battleships (*Idaho*, *Tennessee*, *Texas*, *Arkansas*, and *New York*), along with four heavy cruisers, a light cruiser, and escorts—departed for Iwo Jima. Following the prescribed route, they arrived off the island at 0600 on February 16, 1945. At 0707, *Nevada* fired the first salvo against the Japanese defenders, heralding the beginning of the operation.

While an initial bombardment of the island had commenced, poor weather conditions limited its effectiveness, resulting in largely intermittent fire. However, as conditions improved on February 17 (D-Day minus 2), the barrage of Iwo Jima began in earnest. By 0911, *Nevada*, joined by *Tennessee* and *Idaho*, was positioned 3,000 yards off the beach, unleashing her formidable arsenal on designated targets. Late in the day, *Nevada* demonstrated her versatility when a line of gunboats supporting swimmer reconnaissance came under heavy fire from shore batteries. The battleship engaged the offending battery for two hours, eventually silencing it.

On D-Day, February 19, 1945, *Nevada*, along with *California*, was tasked with providing naval gunfire support for the Fifth Marines' assault on Iwo Jima. Around 0925, as *Nevada* executed her assigned rolling barrage, spotters observed that rounds from her secondary battery were ineffective against a concrete blockhouse. In response, the target was reassigned to the ship's 14-inch main battery. The resulting bombardment exposed a previously concealed blockhouse behind Red Beach 1 by removing the sand obscuring it.

At 1100, when the blockhouse was observed returning fire, *Nevada* unleashed armor-piercing shells, demolishing the target. Later, at 1512, the battleship's crew spotted a gun firing from a cave east of the landing beaches. Leveling her 14-inch guns for direct fire, *Nevada* discharged two rounds. The resulting hit at the cave's mouth blew out the side of the cliff, destroying the enemy gun. Throughout the engagement, *Nevada* was straddled by enemy fire on several occasions but, remarkably, did not sustain any hits.

As night fell, Japanese troops on the island mounted a counterattack, attempting to link up with forces on Mount Suribachi. In support of the forces ashore, *Nevada* fired star shells throughout the night, forcing the Japanese to seek cover and effectively breaking up the counterattack. The battleship's contribution to the Iwo Jima operation continued until March 7, when she was withdrawn at 1800. *Nevada* then departed with TG 52.29.12, arriving at Ulithi on March 10 to prepare for Operation Iceberg, the assault on Okinawa in the Ryukyu Islands.

On March 21, 1945, TF 54, the gunfire and covering force under RAdm. Deyo, left the anchorage at Ulithi and set course for Okinawa. Unit 3, consisting of *Nevada*, *Tennessee*, the heavy cruiser *Wichita*, the light cruisers *Birmingham* and *St. Louis*, and five destroyers, arrived off the island on March 24 and initiated the preinvasion bombardment.

Three days into the bombardment, on March 27 at 0622, *Nevada* faced her first kamikaze attack when an Aichi D3A Type 99 carrier bomber (Val) crashed into the ship. The impact killed eleven crew members and wounded forty-nine others. The attack also damaged turret III, three 20 mm mounts, and one of the ship's Kingfisher observation planes. Despite this blow, *Nevada* held her position in the gunline, a testament to her crew's determination and the ship's resilience.

At 1615 on the same day, a poignant funeral service was held aboard *Nevada* for the ten enlisted men and one officer killed in the kamikaze attack. In a remarkable display of respect and humanity, the ship's chaplain, Marion Stephenson, included the Japanese pilot in his eulogy, saying, "While we as a nation can neither understand nor condone the strange philosophy of the

Following her overhaul at Norfolk Navy Yard, *Nevada* left that facility in early November 1944, bound for the Pacific via the Panama Canal. She is seen here underway in the Pacific on December 5, 1944. *National Archives*

Japanese kamikaze, we as soldiers and sailors can understand the devotion to duty and unflinching disregard for personal consequences which the enemy has shown. And to God, who made us all and will judge us all, is left this man alongside our own."

On D-Day, April 1, *Nevada* took up her bombardment position off Hagushi Beach on Okinawa's western shore. Tasked with providing naval gunfire support for the battle-hardened First Marine Division, she opened fire at 0540, unleashing her arsenal on Japanese airfields, shore defenses, supply dumps, and troop concentrations throughout the operation.

The intensity of the battle around Okinawa was relentless. On April 5, 1945, at 1742, a 6-inch round from a Japanese shore battery struck *Nevada*'s main deck on the port side aft. The battleship's main battery responded with direct fire, her spotters targeting the enemy muzzle flashes. Just four minutes later, at 1746, another Japanese shell found its mark, striking the starboard side of the second deck. This round penetrated five bulkheads before exploding in a portside damage control compartment, where nineteen men were stationed. Two were killed instantly, and the other seventeen were wounded.

The barrage continued with three more hits in quick succession, damaging *Nevada*'s stern crane, aft SG radar, and several 20 mm mounts. Some of the ship's blister compartments were also flooded. Undeterred, *Nevada* responded with her 14-inch guns, silencing the enemy battery after expending seventy-one rounds.

The following morning, April 6, *Nevada* left for Kerama Retto to transfer the bodies of the two men killed by Japanese shellfire for burial ashore. The process of taking on ammunition at Kerama Retto proved to be frustratingly slow and perilous. With the ship's cranes and booms out of commission due to battle damage, crews had to manually move the heavy shells. Each 14-inch shell weighed nearly three-quarters of a ton, and the powder bags approached 100 pounds each, making for backbreaking work. All the while, the work crews maintained constant vigilance against the threat of kamikaze attacks, since Japanese planes were being shot down all around them.

When *Nevada* finally got underway again, her decks were still covered with 14-inch shells and powder cans waiting to be stowed below. The ship's return to action was hampered by mechanical issues. On Sunday, April 8, en route to Kerama Retto, the port engine had to be stopped due to dangerously low tolerances in the turbines. *Nevada* limped into port on her starboard engine alone.

From January 23 to February 10, 1945, USS *Nevada* was temporarily based at Ulithi. During that period the ship's crew prepared for the forthcoming landings at Iwo Jima, with heavy emphasis on gunnery practice. *Nevada*'s Measure 31a, Design 6B camouflage is particularly well defined in this photo of the ship at Ulithi, in the Caroline Islands, on February 6. The photo was taken from the flight deck of the escort carrier USS *Sargent Bay* (CVE-83). *National Archives*

Despite these setbacks, *Nevada* continued to play a crucial role in the Okinawa Campaign. On April 12, she faced a long nightmare of kamikaze attacks—sixteen separate raids before dawn and sporadic activity thereafter. At 1451, *Nevada* joined other ships in firing on a kamikaze headed straight for *Tennessee*, RAdm. Deyo's flagship. The gunners watched in horror as the plane slammed into the battleship, narrowly missing the admiral on the bridge.

On April 13, sad news arrived from home: President Franklin Delano Roosevelt had died at his retreat in Warm Springs, Georgia. However, the war continued unabated. Enemy aircraft began attacking at 0255 and kept coming through the night. *Nevada* continued her shore bombardment during these attacks, breaking off at 0605 to head to Kerama Retto to offload ammunition.

With turret 3 inoperative and other systems experiencing problems, it was finally time for *Nevada* to head east for repairs. After transferring her remaining ammunition, she headed back to Okinawa to fire illumination rounds urgently requested by a shore fire control party to help repel a Japanese banzai charge. At 0819 on April 14, *Nevada*, in company with *Maryland*, *Pensacola*, fifteen transports, and seven escorts, left Okinawa and headed for home.

Nevada reached Pearl Harbor on May 2, 1945, where she underwent overhaul and repair. She also received additional antiaircraft armament in preparation for the expected invasion of the Japanese home islands. Drydock work was completed on May 12, and *Nevada* moved to a nearby pier. Once yard work was finished, sea trials began on June 1, with her full-power speed recorded at 18.7 knots—a clear indication that age was catching up with the venerable battleship.

On June 11, *Nevada* steamed for the bypassed Japanese garrison on the island of Emidji in the Jaluit atoll. Arriving off the island early on June 18, *Nevada*, accompanied by the destroyers *Murray* and *Taylor*, maneuvered to a range of 9,000 yards and began to bombard the island. After silencing the Japanese counterbattery fire, *Nevada* closed to 4,000 yards and methodically raked the island, destroying her designated targets in progression.

Nevada joined *California* and *West Virginia* on June 30, 1945, for operations in the East China Sea. The battleships, as part of TF 32, were to provide cover for minesweeping operations preparatory to the invasion of Japan. On July 6, a squadron of enemy Mitsubishi Ki-46 Type 100 command reconnaissance planes ("Dinah") approached the task force but were driven off by Navy fighters.

On July 22, *Nevada* received orders to detach from TF 32 and proceed north to join TF 95 for an attack by naval aircraft on a Japanese naval base near Shanghai, China. She was subsequently joined by the large cruisers *Guam* and *Alaska*, both of which requested aid from *Nevada*'s medical staff on July 28.

Nevada returned to Buckner Bay, Okinawa, for replenishment on July 31. She then sortied with the large cruisers for a return to operations in the East China Sea until they were relieved and ordered to Leyte Gulf, Philippines, on August 7. *Nevada* slipped her berth the next day and departed Buckner Bay, to be replaced by *Pennsylvania*, which was hit by a Japanese aerial torpedo within hours of her arrival. On August 15, within days of reaching Samar in Leyte Gulf, *Nevada*'s crew received word that the Japanese had surrendered.

World War II was over. *Nevada* received orders to return to Buckner Bay, where she remained as the Japanese signed the articles of surrender aboard *Missouri* in Tokyo Bay on September 2, 1945. While there, her men sat out to restore *Nevada* to her full prewar splendor. As part of wartime camouflage, nearly every surface of the ship had been painted. Now that covering could be removed from her teakwood decks and brass fixtures.

Taken moments from the preceding photo from USS *Sargent Bay*, the escort carrier comes dangerously close to *Nevada* at Ulithi, resulting in a near collision. *National Archives*

Nevada was photographed from off her port stern by a photographer aboard USS *Sargent Bay* at Ulithi on February 6, 1945. Although *Nevada*'s camouflage paint was only a couple of months old, it shows signs of heavy weathering. Numerous paint touch-ups are visible on the aft part of the hull. The Vought OS2U-3 Kingfisher observation planes have three-color camouflage (Sea Blue, Intermediate Blue, and Insignia White), and the plane on the catapult bears the number 11 on the fuselage. *National Archives*

USS *Nevada* is observed from her aft-port quarter at Ulithi on February 6, 1945. *Nevada* would depart from Ulithi four days later, February 10, bound for the invasion of Iwo Jima. *National Archives*

Three days after departing from Ulithi, *Nevada* (*foreground*) is conducting an underway replenishment (UNREP), using a highline to transfer ammunition to the destroyer USS *Van Valkenbergh* (DD-656). To the far left is a partial view of the port Mk. 37 secondary-battery director, with the shutters of the vision ports opened. *National Archives*

Crewmen at the center of the photo are preparing to send a bagful of supplies over to *Van Valkenbergh* by a highline. At the bottom left, painted in white around the inside of the splinter shield of a quadruple 40 mm gun mount, are numbers of an azimuth scale, in 15-degree increments. *National Archives*

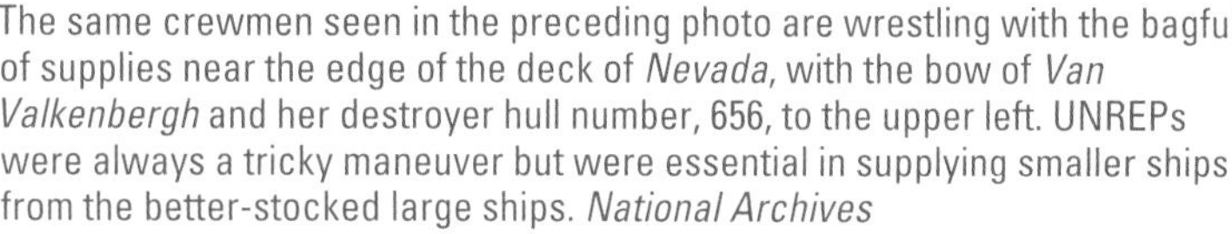

The same crewmen seen in the preceding photo are wrestling with the bagful of supplies near the edge of the deck of *Nevada*, with the bow of *Van Valkenbergh* and her destroyer hull number, 656, to the upper left. UNREPs were always a tricky maneuver but were essential in supplying smaller ships from the better-stocked large ships. *National Archives*

En route to Iwo Jima from Ulithi, *Nevada* conducted practice operations for the imminent invasion, off Saipan, on February 13, 1945. Here, one of *Nevada*'s Vought OS2U-3 Kingfishers has just been launched from the catapult on that date. *National Archives*

As part of Task Force 54, *Nevada* joined other battleships in bombarding Iwo Jima beginning on February 16, 1945, three days before D-Day. With their powerful main-battery guns and excellent spotting from their observation planes, the US battleships were able to shell Japanese defenses with surgical skill. In a photo taken from USS *Texas* (BB-35), *Nevada* (*left*) and the cruiser USS *Biloxi* (CL-80) are shelling Japanese positions on Iwo Jima on February 16. *National Archives*

Her main battery trained to starboard, USS *Nevada* has just released a salvo against Japanese positions on Iwo Jima on D-Day, February 19, 1945. In the left background is the battleship USS *Washington* (BB-56). *National Archives*

Spotters are busy on the lookout station above the pilothouse of *Nevada* during a bombardment against Japanese strongpoints on Iwo Jima. In the forward position is a sky lookout. The large helmet on the crewman next to the man with the chart board in front of him is a talker's helmet, which was spacious enough to fit over an intercom headset. On the pedestal in the foreground is a target designator transmitter and receiver. The cylindrical structure to the left is the base of the forward Mk. 37 secondary-battery director. Above its door are aircraft-recognition charts for Japanese (*upper*) and US planes. *National Archives*

This photo of *Nevada* during a shore bombardment of Iwo Jima was taken from the same perspective as the preceding photo. At the top are the three shutters for the vision ports on the front of the forward Mk. 37 director in their open positions. *National Archives*

The 14-inch guns of turret 3 of *Nevada* have just fired a salvo at enemy positions on Iwo Jima on D-Day, February 19, 1945. On that morning, *Nevada*'s two observation planes launched at 0640, and her guns commenced firing at 0700. *National Archives*

A photographer aboard *Nevada* took this view of the invasion beaches at Iwo Jima before the landings. Two small ships are underway offshore as smoke roils up off the beach. To the left is Mount Suribachi. *National Archives*

Off Iwo Jima on D-plus-3, February 22, 1944, *Nevada* is maneuvering to recover one of its Vought Kingfishers. To prepare for the recovery, the ship has made a turn to port, which acted to create a relatively calm patch of ocean that was safe for the floatplane to touch down on. On the roof of turret 3 are floating nets.
National Archives

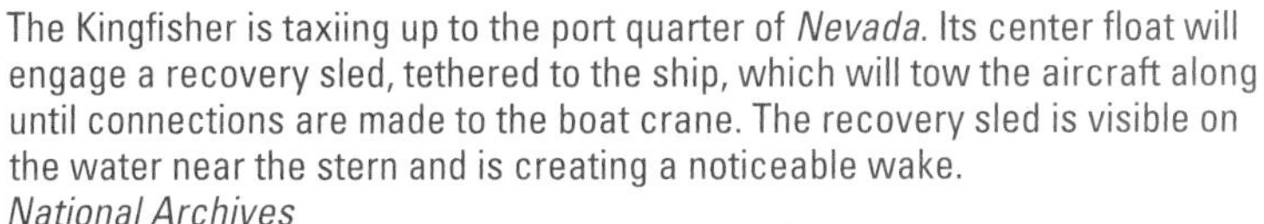

The Kingfisher is taxiing up to the port quarter of *Nevada*. Its center float will engage a recovery sled, tethered to the ship, which will tow the aircraft along until connections are made to the boat crane. The recovery sled is visible on the water near the stern and is creating a noticeable wake.
National Archives

A wounded sailor on a stretcher is being transferred from *Nevada* to a hospital ship off Iwo Jima, on February 25, 1945. This was likely one of the wounded crewmen of *LCI-441* who had been brought aboard *Nevada* for medical treatment on February 18 after that landing craft came under Japanese fire. Those crewmen were transferred from *Nevada* to the evacuation transport USS *Pinckney* (APH-2) on February 25.
National Archives

Mount Suribachi and ships of the US Fleet are in the distance in this view taken from the forward 36-inch searchlight platform of *Nevada* on March 6, 1945. To the far right is a partial view of the forward Mk. 37 director, also called Sky 1. On the following day, *Nevada* would depart from Iwo Jima to Ulithi, for resupply and repairs to the ship and relaxation for the crew. *National Archives*

USS *Nevada* is underway off an unidentified coastline around March 1945. She is wearing Measure 31a, Design 6B camouflage. Both of the battleship's Kingfisher observation planes are embarked.

Following a brief respite at Ulithi, *Nevada* departed with Task Group 54.2 for Okinawa, where the group would lend fire support to the US invasion of that island. This photo of the battle line steaming toward Okinawa was taken from *Nevada*. Within a few days, the area of the ship pictured here would be the scene of great devastation from a kamikaze plane. *National Archives*

Almost as soon as *Nevada* came on station off Okinawa, on March 26, 1945, she came under attack from Japanese submarines and aircraft. Here, one of the quadruple 40 mm gun mounts fires at a target. Spent ammunition casings litter the gun platform. The crewman in the foreground is manning a sky lookout. Above his helmet, situated inside a curved splinter shield, are two crewmen wearing helmets, manning a Mk. 51 director. These directors remotely controlled the firing of the 40 mm gun batteries. *National Archives*

Less than a day after *Nevada* came on station off Okinawa, at 6:22 on the morning of March 27, a lone kamikaze pilot crashed his plane into the aft part of the main deck. The crash area was photographed moments after the impact, with several small fires burning on the deck. Nine crewmen were killed immediately, and forty-seven were badly wounded. *National Archives*

The devastation caused by the suicide pilot is seen after the fires were extinguished. Fire hoses are lying on the deck. In the foreground is a wrecked splinter shield. To the far right is the barbette of turret 3, to the immediate rear of which is turret 4.

Crewmen clean up debris from a devastated 20 mm gun position on *Nevada* following the kamikaze attack. A 20 mm gun mount and shield, minus the cannon, is toward the lower part of the photo. The view was from the roof of turret 3.

A *Nevada* crewman lifts a ceremonial Japanese flag carried by the kamikaze pilot, whose remains lie against the ventilator in the right background. At the top are the guns of turret 4.

The mangled remains of the suicide pilot lie on the deck aft of turret 3. *National Archives*

The remains of the suicide pilot were given a dignified burial at sea in the aftermath of the March 27 kamikaze attack. Standing next to turret 4, Chaplain Marion Stephenson delivers the service before the burial. *National Archives*

Wounded crewmen are being transferred from *Nevada* to a smaller craft, for transport to a hospital ship, in the aftermath of the March 27 kamikaze strike. Two of the wounded crewmen subsequently died. *National Archives*

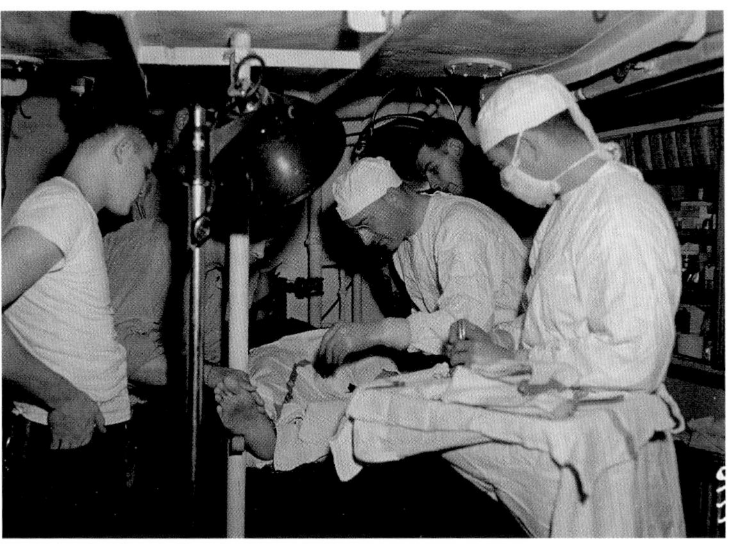

In a battle-dressing station in USS *Nevada*, a surgeon, Cmdr. N. E. Bear, *center*, prepares to amputate the leg of a wounded crewman. *Nevada*'s limited medical facilities were stressed to the maximum during the treatment of the many crewmen wounded in the attack. *National Archives*

Empty ammunition containers for storing 14-inch, 5-inch, and 40 mm ammunition are being transferred from *Nevada* (*lower left*) to the deck of a landing ship, tank (LST) off Okinawa sometime before April 27, 1944. The cylindrical units were powder tanks, for transporting and storing powder charges; the boxes were for storing 40 mm cartridges. The sheer number of powder tanks and ammo boxes is a testimony to the heavy expenditure of ammunition during the ship's service off Okinawa. In the right background is a hospital ship. *National Archives*

In a photo taken around April 1945 to the starboard of turret 3, in the foreground is a temporary patch on the main deck. The patch was several inches above the surrounding deck. Stacked in the background are powder tanks for 5-inch guns (*left*) and storage boxes for 40 mm ammunition (*right*). *National Archives*

This series of photos documents damage to USS *Nevada*'s turret 3 from the kamikaze strike of March 27. Shrapnel dug pits, including some deep ones, into the thick armor of the barbette. *National Archives*

Further details of shrapnel damage to turret 3 are pictured. *National Archives*

Some shrapnel pits are on the frontal armor of turret 3. Several crewmen inside the turret were injured from shrapnel that penetrated through the space between the gun tubes and the frontal armor. *National Archives*

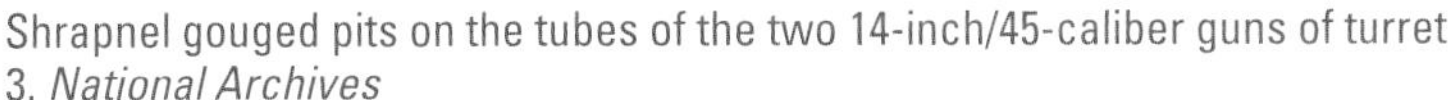

Shrapnel gouged pits on the tubes of the two 14-inch/45-caliber guns of turret 3. *National Archives*

Shrapnel gouges peppered the tube of the left 14-inch/45-caliber gun on turret 3. In May 1945 the guns of turret 3 would be replaced. To the lower right is the left rangefinder hood of turret 4. *National Archives*

On April 5, 1945, while shelling Japanese positions on Okinawa, *Nevada* came under fire from Japanese artillery ashore. Five shells struck the battleship, including one that penetrated the port blister at the waterline, as seen here. Above the hole is the ledge at the top of the blister. The access panel on the ledge at the far right has been removed; visible inside is the top of the belt armor. *National Archives*

While the Okinawa Campaign raged on, *Nevada* departed for Pearl Harbor for repairs, arriving there on April 30. She is seen here, facing aft on the starboard side of the main deck, in drydock the following day. A notation on the photo indicates where the part of a splinter shield destroyed in the kamikaze attack was removed. The 20 mm gun mount near the center of the photo is positioned behind what was left of the splinter shield. *National Archives*

Pockmarks from shrapnel are visible on close inspection on the 14-inch gun, the gunhouse, and the barbette of turret 3 in this photo of *Nevada* from the starboard side in drydock on May 2, 1945. The previously seen temporary patch on the deck is present in the lower center of the photo. To the inboard side of the patch is a deck winch. *National Archives*

Sailors are departing *Nevada*, and others are bringing aboard supplies on a gangway on the port side of the battleship, in drydock at Pearl Harbor on May 1, 1945. A pedestal mount for a 20 mm gun is inside the splinter shield, as are oxyacetylene bottles on a rack. *National Archives*

The starboard deck winch, on the main deck to the side of space between turrets 3 and 4, was damaged by shrapnel in the March 27 kamikaze attack. It is seen facing forward in a photo taken in drydock at Pearl Harbor on May 1, 1945. *National Archives*

The previously pictured entry hole in the port blister of *Nevada* from a projectile fired by Japanese shore artillery is slightly below the center of this photo, taken in drydock on May 1, 1945. A chalk mark on the blister indicates the location of frame 109. *National Archives*

After repairs on *Nevada* were completed at Pearl Harbor in late May 1945, the ship was subjected to sea trials, weapons trials, and crew training off Oahu in early June. On June 7, crewmen are unpacking a Radioplane TDD radio-controlled drone aircraft, for use as a target in antiaircraft gunnery practice, below the big guns of turret 4. On the deck just aft of those guns is a newly installed twin 20 mm gun mount. *National Archives*

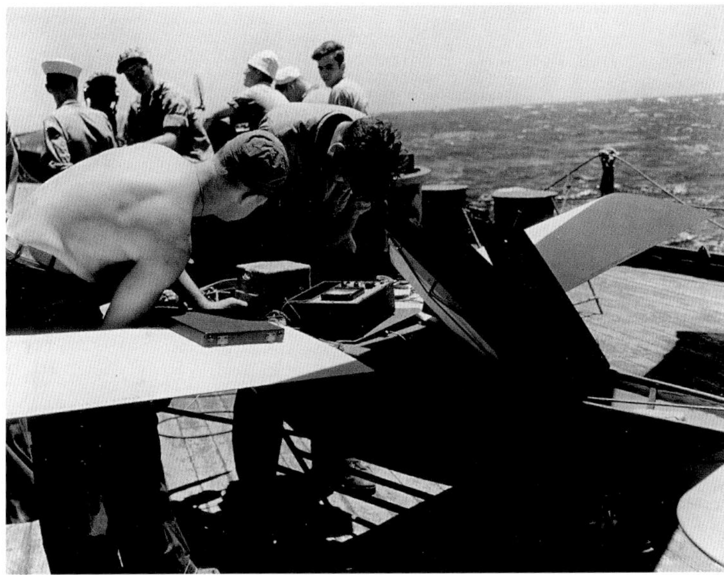

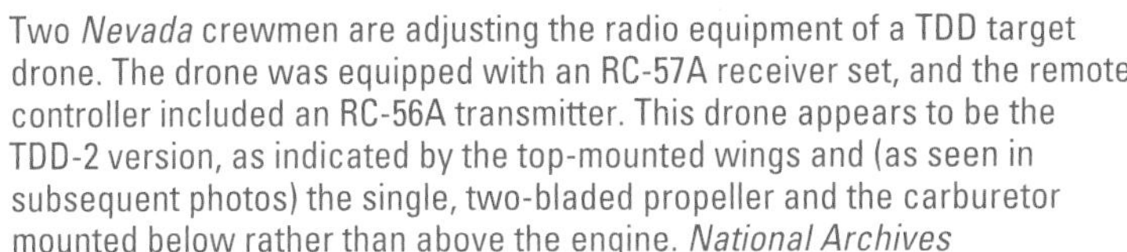

Two *Nevada* crewmen are adjusting the radio equipment of a TDD target drone. The drone was equipped with an RC-57A receiver set, and the remote controller included an RC-56A transmitter. This drone appears to be the TDD-2 version, as indicated by the top-mounted wings and (as seen in subsequent photos) the single, two-bladed propeller and the carburetor mounted below rather than above the engine. *National Archives*

The TDD-2 is being mounted on the catapult for launching. The drone had upswept wings, clearly seen from this perspective. To the right is the aircraft crane. *National Archives*

The TDD-2 is installed on the catapult and ready for launching. The carburetor, mounted to the front of the fuselage and under the two-cylinder engine, is in view. A tubular frame held the drone to the launching car until takeoff was achieved. *National Archives*

On June 7, 1945, a TDD-2 is being launched from the catapult of *Nevada*. Once the launching car reaches the end of the catapult and hits the buffers on the catapult, the drone will separate from its support frame and go airborne. *National Archives*

The 14-inch guns of turret 4 are at the lower left as a TDD-2 drone flies off the catapult, seen at the far left. The TDD-2 had a maximum speed of 102 miles per hour. *National Archives*

Following her repairs at Pearl Harbor, USS *Nevada* returned to the seat of war in the western Pacific. She is seen at anchor in Buckner Bay, Okinawa, during the summer of 1945. At Pearl Harbor, the ship had been repainted; judging by the overall dark color of the ship in this and subsequent photos, the camouflage scheme appears to have been Measure 21 (1945 Revision), with Navy Gray on all vertical surfaces and Deck Gray on the decks. (However, subsequent photos indicate that *Nevada*'s wooden decks are a light color; they may have been unpainted or finished in a lighter color than Deck Gray). *National Archives*

CHAPTER 10

Nevada's Final Chapter

As summer gave way to autumn in 1945, *Nevada*'s war service was drawing to a close. On September 16, the battle-hardened vessel weathered a fierce typhoon, a final test of her seaworthiness after years of combat. A week later, on September 23, *Nevada* set course for Pearl Harbor. Her decks were crowded with soldiers and Marines eager to return home, the ship packed to capacity with the human cargo of victory.

Nevada's wartime record stood as a testament to her crew's dedication and the ship's resilience. Since the outbreak of hostilities, she had steamed an impressive 137,027 miles and spent 389 days in combat areas. Her guns had spoken often and with devastating effect, firing more than five thousand rounds from her 14-inch main battery and an astounding 18,000 rounds from her 5-inch secondary armament. These statistics, while impressive, only hinted at the true measure of *Nevada*'s contribution to the war effort.

The human cost and valor of *Nevada*'s service were reflected in the numerous decorations awarded to her crew. Among the ship's company, two sailors received the Medal of Honor, the nation's highest military decoration. Fifteen crew members were awarded the Navy Cross, the service's second-highest honor. The Silver Star, awarded for gallantry in action, was bestowed upon two of *Nevada*'s sailors, while ten received the Bronze Star for heroic or meritorious achievement.

The toll of combat was evident in the approximately 240 Purple Hearts awarded to *Nevada*'s crew, each representing a sailor wounded in the line of duty. Additional decorations included one Air Medal, three Navy and Marine Corps Medals, and two letters of commendation from the secretary of the Navy. These awards painted a vivid picture of the bravery and sacrifice that had become hallmarks of *Nevada*'s war service.

On October 9, 1945, *Nevada* departed Pearl Harbor for her home port of San Pedro, California. As she left Hawaiian waters, she participated in a poignant ceremony. A line of six battleships, ranging from *Arkansas*, the oldest in the fleet, to *Iowa*, one of the newest, passed in review off the coast of Honolulu. Crews manned the rails in dress white uniforms, a stirring sight that symbolized the passing of an era in naval warfare.

Nevada's journey home continued without incident. In the early hours of Monday, October 15, at 0222, her radar reported land 96 miles east. As dawn broke, the familiar silhouettes of Santa Rosa and San Nicholas Islands came into view at 0545. For the crew, many of whom had spent years away from home, these landmarks heralded their imminent return.

At 1506, *Nevada* once again rounded the San Pedro breakwater, dropping anchor in Berth 231. For many of her crew, this marked the end of their service aboard the venerable battleship. They disembarked, stepping onto American soil for the first time in years, their thoughts undoubtedly a mix of relief, pride, and uncertainty about the future.

Among those leaving *Nevada* for the last time was Captain Grosskopf, who had guided the ship through some of her most challenging moments. Command of *Nevada* passed to Capt. Cecil C. Adell, who was to be her final commanding officer.

On Monday, October 29, while moored at Berth 13, Pier 1, Terminal Island, Long Beach, *Nevada* received orders to report to the commander of Service Force Pacific Fleet (ComServPac) for Magic Carpet duty—a program to shuttle servicemen home on warships.

At 1554 on October 30, *Nevada* was once again underway for Pearl Harbor on her first Magic Carpet voyage, tying up at Berth H-3 at Pearl on November 5. The next day, after taking on over a thousand returning servicemen, she steamed for Seattle.

Nevada anchored at Berth 6, Tacoma, on November 14, and the next day tied up first at Pier 2 there, then moved to Berth E, Seattle, that afternoon.

On Sunday, November 18, she left Washington, again steaming for Pearl Harbor, where she moored at Berth H-2 at 0954 on Sunday, November 25. That afternoon, having taken on more passengers and fuel, she left at 1625 en route to San Pedro, where she arrived on the afternoon of Saturday, December 1. She entered Dry Dock 1 at Terminal Island at 1457 and remained there until Friday, December 7. Successful trial runs were made that day, and the next day she again steamed for Pearl Harbor, arriving once more at Berth H-3 at 1046 on Friday, December 14. She left again for San Pedro at 1624 that same day, completing this, her final Magic Carpet voyage, at 1451 on December 20, when she anchored at Berth O-2 in San Pedro Harbor, moving again to Pier 231 on Saturday.

As the new year began, the ever-diminishing crew of *Nevada* set out to offload the ship. Tons of antiaircraft guns, ammunition, parts, and supplies were offloaded for future use elsewhere.

But in February, this process was reversed when the ship was assigned for use in the Operation Crossroads atomic-weapon experiments. The tests were to subject ships and equipment to atomic blasts under warlike conditions, which for *Nevada* meant having 1,500 tons of ammunition, 66 percent of its wartime load for her 14-inch, 5-inch, 40 mm, and 20 mm guns. Also aboard was a host of other provisions. Her orders stated that *Nevada* was to be loaded with "Fuel oil 33.3 percent, Diesel oil 50 percent, Ammunition 66 2/3 percent, Potable and reserve feed water 95 percent, Salt water ballast 1850."

A myriad of scientific equipment and test samples were also placed aboard, and to accommodate this, four of her 5-inch/38-caliber mounts were removed. Among the material placed aboard were seven "armor plates and samples of known ballistic, chemical and metallurgical properties representing current manufacture of all types and gauges [*sic*]."

Four of these were heavy plates, which required "shoring the area under the plates for two deck levels in order to provide adequate shock resistant supports for the heavy weight plates."

The samples were secured with "heavy steel corner pieces welded to steel decks with heavy steel securing clips welded to corner pieces with clip and samples separated by wood and asbestos fillers" and were in place for both tests.

It was intended that following the test named Able, "three metallurgical samples from each of the first four plates . . . were returned to the Naval Proving Grounds, Dahlgren, after the test for a comprehensive metallurgical examination in order to determine any effects caused by Test 'A.'"

A variety of Army gear was secured to Nevada's decks, with the orders stating, "All armored vehicles were secured to the deck by rods or turnbuckles from the towing links on the tanks to pad eyes on the deck," and all tank hatches were closed and locked for the tests. The vehicles and gear placed aboard, and their locations, were as follows:

Description	Deck	Frame	Side
90 mm Motor Carriage M36	main	116–121	P
M26 Tank	main	109–115	S
M24 Tank	upper	38	S
Half Track M16	upper	42–46	P
105 mm Howitzer M2A2	main	95	P
155 mm Gun M1A1	main	110	p
40 mm Gun M2A2	main	95	S
75 mm Gun (AC) M10	main	121	P
90 mm Gun (AA) M2	main	120	S
Director M9A1	main	111	S
Generating Unit M7A1	main	117½	S
Cable System M1	main	119½	P
1⁄4-Ton Truck 4×4	upper	40	S
Cargo Carrier M29C	upper	43	S
Truck Auto Repair M8A1	main	130	P
2½-Ton Amphibian Truck	main	128	P
4.5" Rocket Launcher	main	125	P
Height Finder M1	main	100	P
Light Armored Car M8	upper	37	P

After VJ-Day, marking the end of World War II, *Nevada* remained in the western Pacific for another month, after which she returned to Pearl Harbor. She is seen here off Oahu on October 9, 1945, as she began a voyage to the US West Coast. A Vought Kingfisher is mounted on the catapult. *National Archives*

Nevada is steaming off the coast of Oahu on October 9, 1945. Crewmen in their dress whites are manning the rails. The light-colored wooden decks are apparent in this aerial photo of *Nevada* departing from Oahu on October 9, 1945. Before departing from waters off Oahu, *Nevada* and five other battleships passed in review, with crews lining the rails in dress whites. *National Archives*

A variety of Army and Navy ammunition was also subjected to the tests, some of which was on pallets bolted to the decks, others stowed in magazines and ammunition-handling compartments or in the loading trays for the guns.

For the first test, Able, an airburst of an atomic bomb 500 feet above the fleet, *Nevada* was selected to be *the* target, and for this purpose she got a new paint job—International Orange.

At 1130 on May 1, 1946, she left California for the last time, steaming to Pearl Harbor, tying up once more at Berth F-8 on May 8. With her fuel bunkers topped off with 257,000 gallons of fuel, and her decks cluttered with Army gear placed aboard for evaluation, and with a reduced crew of 403 officers and men, she steamed independently for Bikini Atoll on May 20. Arriving there on May 28, she tied up to buoys 13 and 14.

At Bikini, Seabees had constructed various recreational facilities for the men assigned to the project, including two bars.

The crew of the B-29 "Dave's Dream" were selected to deliver the ordnance. A rehearsal exercise, code-named Queen Day, was planned for June 23, although weather forced it to be postponed until June 24. For this, the men aboard *Nevada* set condition Zed and secured all equipment except for a diesel generator that supplied a radar beacon and searchlight, both intended to guide the bomber to its target. The day prior to the rehearsal, the crew was evacuated to the support ship USS *George Clymer*, except for Capt. Adell, four officers, and three enlisted men, who left the ship at 0415 on the morning of the rehearsal.

Test Able was scheduled for July 1, and once again the day prior the crew was evacuated but for Capt. Adell, four officers, and four enlisted men, who did not leave the ship until 0400 the day of the test.

As reported in *Bombs at Bikini: The Official Report of Operation Crossroads*, the day began with a final practice run:

> The final practice run, a full-rehearsal run, began at 8:20 a.m. A radar beacon at Bikini was picked up from a distance of 50 miles and was used to time the approach and maintain the desired course of 45 degrees true. The Bomb Commander and his two weaponeers made last minute adjustments to bomb and bombsight. A flashing lamp on the [USS] NEVADA came into view; NEVADA'S high-visibility paint was clearly identified. The simulated practice drop was made at 8:31 a.m.
>
> The final run began at 8:50 a.m., from a distance of more than 50 miles. Course and altitude were held constant. Visibility

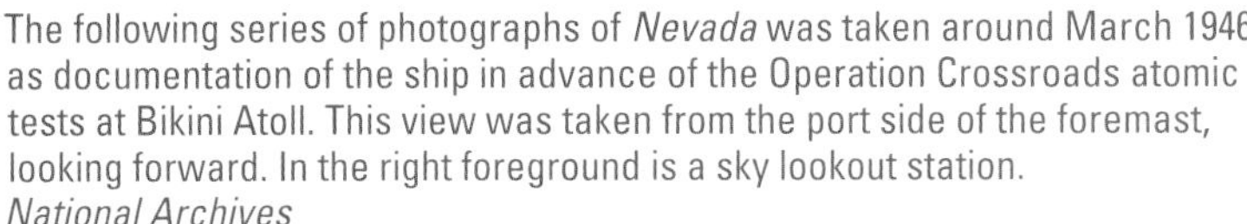

The following series of photographs of *Nevada* was taken around March 1946, as documentation of the ship in advance of the Operation Crossroads atomic tests at Bikini Atoll. This view was taken from the port side of the foremast, looking forward. In the right foreground is a sky lookout station. *National Archives*

The forward part of *Nevada* is observed from the starboard side of the mainmast. Two sky lookouts, complete with cushioned seats, are positioned in the foreground. At the top left is the right side of Sky 1, or the forward Mk. 37 director. *National Archives*

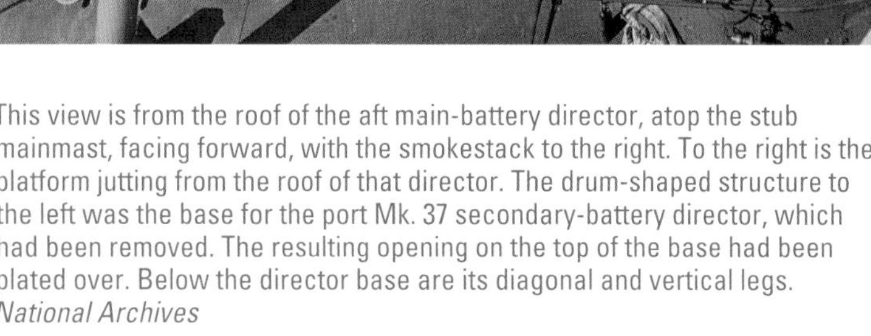
This view is from the roof of the aft main-battery director, atop the stub mainmast, facing forward, with the smokestack to the right. To the right is the platform jutting from the roof of that director. The drum-shaped structure to the left was the base for the port Mk. 37 secondary-battery director, which had been removed. The resulting opening on the top of the base had been plated over. Below the director base are its diagonal and vertical legs. *National Archives*

The base for the starboard Mk. 37 director and its tubular legs, *right*, are viewed from the platform on the top of the aft main-battery director. Between and to the front of the smokestack and the Mk. 37 director is the starboard leg of the foremast, with ladder rungs on it. *National Archives*

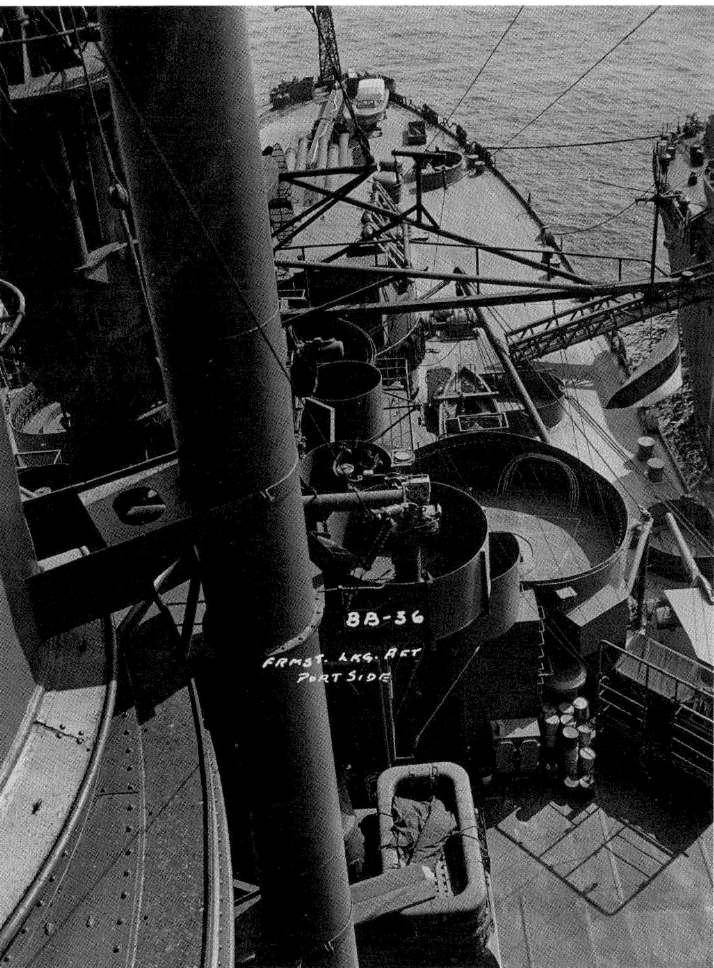

The aft starboard sector of *Nevada* is seen from her foremast. Three round splinter shields and platforms for quadruple 40 mm gun mounts are in view; the guns mounts have been removed from them. In the two armored tubs to the left of the starboard leg of the mainmast (*right*) are a Mk. 51 director (*nearest to the camera*) and a sky lookout. To the upper right is the aft main-battery control and spotting station. *National Archives*

The smokestack is to the left in this view facing aft from the mainmast. To the right of the stack, near the center of the photo, are tubs containing a sky lookout and a Mk. 51 director. A motorboat is stored on the fantail to the port side of the catapult.

The aft part of the main deck is seen from the mainmast. At the bottom center are the Mk. 12 and Mk. 22 "orange peel" antennas above the aft Mk. 37 director. Below the antennas are two tubs from which quadruple 40 mm gun mounts had been removed. At the rear of the deck, 20 mm gun mounts and shields are still in place inside the tubs, but the guns have been dismounted. *National Archives*

> was excellent. Within a few seconds of 9:00 a.m., the bomb was released and the bombardier called "Bomb away, bomb away!"
>
> Bomb bay doors were then closed, and the plane made a 150-degree level turn to the left. It made a shallow dive, losing 1,000 feet altitude while increasing speed of get-away.
>
> During the first few seconds of the bomb's descent, the bomb's course was almost parallel to that of the plane itself, and its velocity too was essentially the same (roughly 300 miles per hour). The downward velocity of the bomb increased rapidly at this point.
>
> The target, enjoying its last few seconds of normal existence, was the most gigantic test target ever assembled.

Incredibly, although delivered by the highest-scoring bomber crew for accuracy in multiple tests, they missed, with the bomb, code-named "Gilda," exploding 1,500 feet off target. At 1430, after radiation monitors had entered the lagoon and reported that radiation levels were as expected, VAdm. William Blandy, commander of Joint Army-Navy Task Force 1 and overseer of Operation Crossroads, approved reentry to Bikini Atoll.

One observer noted that "the fleet looked as though it had returned from a quick trip to hell." At 1430 on July 3—two days after the Able blast, a nineteen-man inspection party boarded *Nevada*, finding her topsides in shambles. Radar and radio antenna had been blown off, and the outer casing of her stack was destroyed, with the inner smoke pipe crimped. The blast-facing side of the superstructure was bent, and the Bureau of Ships recorded damage to her decks, saying, "Forward of the superstructure is deflected between transverse bulkheads. Maximum deflections of four to six inches appear to starboard alongside of No. 1 turret. The deck beams and supporting structure conform to the deflection of the deck and the deck beams are distorted in way of their connections to bulkheads and shell stiffeners."

Damage was worse aft of number 4 turret, with the bureau noting, "This depression pulled the deck away from the after face of No. 4 barbette. The maximum deflection in this area is about 16½ inches. Between frames 122 and 132 the maximum deflection is about 14 inches. The deflections of the main deck are accompanied by failure of supporting stanchions and distortion of connections of the deck beams to the shell stiffeners. The second deck is deflected aft of the armor from bulkhead 122 to about frame 134, the maximum being about 12 inches. The damage diminishes as it goes deeper into the ship."

At 1515, a second boarding party began a detailed survey belowdecks, which indicated the merit of her all-or-nothing armor configuration, with little observable damage beyond dust blown from the ventilators. At 1730, her gunnery officer and ten gunners came aboard and found that her magazines were in acceptable condition. At the same time the gunnery officer came aboard, Capt. Adell and the first boarding party left the ship. It was found that only a few isolated compartments showed signs of flooding, and her draft was the same as before the test. At the end of the day, a seventeen-man security detail and the ship's navigator came aboard to spend the night. Capt. Adell joined them at 2030. Capt. Adell noted in his report, "The overall condition of the ship is good." However, had her crew been aboard, they would not have fared as well. Goat #119, tethered inside a gun turret and shielded by armor plate, received enough fireball radiation to die four days later of radiation sickness, having survived two days longer than goat #53, which was on the deck, unshielded. The Bureau of Ship's report opined that had *Nevada* been fully manned, "the amount of reduction in efficiency due to the high casualty rate among specially trained personnel because of inadequate protection from radiation and air shock, although unpredictable, appears to be of significance."

Starting the next day, *Nevada*'s engineering men labored to get two boilers back in operation. On July 8, *Nevada* was declared to be safe for reboarding (in fact, radiation readings were still dangerously high), and the next day the starboard engine was placed in operation and 81,606 gallons of fuel were taken aboard. *Nevada* was supplying her own power. By July 13 the minor leaks previously mentioned had a caused a 3-degree list, but an underwater inspection by divers found little damage below the waterline.

Test Baker, the detonation of a 23-kiloton "Fat Man" atomic weapon 90 feet below water, was scheduled for Friday, July 25. Because water is incompressible, it was expected that this blast would cause far more damage than did the airburst. Most of the crew had again left the ship by Thursday afternoon, and at 1432, Capt. Adell and the last men left for the *George Clymer*.

Baker was detonated at 0835 on July 25, suspended from the landing ship, medium 60 (*LSM-60*), anchored 1,030 yards from *Nevada*. A 2,000-foot-diameter column of water rose from the blast at the rate of 1 mile per second, an estimated 2 million tons of water, mixed with rock and coral blasted from the floor of the lagoon. The underwater shock wave battered the hull of *Nevada* and the other target ships, their topsides being showered by the highly radioactive water that had been swept up into the column.

After returning to the West Coast in October 1945, *Nevada* made three round trips to Pearl Harbor and back to California under the Magic Carpet program to bring US servicemen back to the States. Subsequently, the battleship lay in port at San Pedro, California, for several months. By early 1946 the Navy had determined to use *Nevada* and several other obsolete warships in the Operation Crossroads atomic-bomb tests at Bikini Atoll that summer. The ship is seen off San Pedro on March 12, 1946, undergoing preparations for the atomic tests. *National Archives*

Nevada is observed from the starboard side off San Pedro on March 12, 1946. The forward and aft twin 5-inch/38-caliber gun mounts were left in place on both sides of the ship, with the other four mounts having been removed. Most or all of the 40 mm and 20 mm guns had been removed. *National Archives*

Barges and a floating crane, *YD-113*, are moored alongside *Nevada*'s port side, in a companion view to the preceding one. Much of the ship's stores and furnishings were removed in advance of the atomic tests.
National Archives

Nevada is viewed from directly above off San Pedro on March 12, 1946. Locations where 5-inch/38-caliber gun mounts were removed from the superstructure are marked by large, round plugs on the deck.
National Archives

In a March 1946 aerial photo of *Nevada* from astern off San Pedro, a 20 mm gun mount with armored shield remains in place in the tub on the starboard side of the stern. The floating crane was loading ammunition from a barge to the battleship; part of the Bikini atomic tests would assess the effects of an atomic blast on a battleship loaded with 1,500 tons of ammunition.
National Archives

ALL HANDS
THE BUREAU OF NAVAL PERSONNEL INFORMATION BULLETIN
1 JULY 1946
ATOMIC BOMB TEST
EXTRA
BIKINI BULLSEYE
See Page 12: A BASIC COURSE IN NUCLEAR PHYSICS

Operation Crossroads not surprisingly garnered a great deal of publicity, and *Nevada*, with her unique International Orange paint scheme, was a natural for coverage of this event, such as the cover of the July 1, 1946, US Navy magazine, *All Hands*. The high-visibility finish was intended to serve as a fail-safe identification aid to the bombardier who would release the atomic bomb. *Nevada* was scheduled to be the target for the bomb drop, anchored in the center of a fleet of target ships.

Immediately after the blast, radio-controlled boats with Geiger counters entered the lagoon, recording radiation levels 80,000 times the maximum allowed for humans. Despite this, by the end of the day, 15,000 men were back aboard ships in the lagoon.

Capt. Adell along with five officers and twenty-seven men reboarded *Nevada* on August 9 at 0745, with sixteen of the men leaving at 1135.

More men came aboard at 1300 and stayed, along with the captain, until 1645.

It was determined that the entire topsides, as well as some spaces belowdecks, were highly radioactive. Despite this, the next day at 0745, Capt. Adell and ninety-one men returned to the ship. They were joined by twenty-three more men at 1015. At 1130, a group of 104 men left the ship, while a group of eighty boarded at 1315. At 1630, Capt. Adell and ninety men left the ship. The ship remained largely vacant until August 17, when once again at 0745, nine men boarded, joined at 0915 by Capt. Adell and 103 more men, and a further eighty-eight at 1215. At 1425, ninety-three of the men left, and at 1715, Capt. Adell and the remainder of the men left the ship.

Inspections of the ship revealed that the forward main battery turrets had been lifted out of the barbettes and dropped back in place, and, according to the Bureau of Ships report, that all "furniture, machinery and miscellaneous equipment not secured are overturned and thrown about, bunks and lockers are down, floor plates are dislodged." The report continued, "The whole topside, decks, bulkheads, waterways, ladders, and ventilators were covered by radioactive spray and water containing sand and coral which was highly radioactive. The ship also was covered by the atomic cloud or vapor. All of these, the radioactive water, spray and atomic cloud, left the ship in a highly radioactive condition. This in itself made the ship dangerous for personnel to live in or remain onboard [*sic*] and even though they may have escaped any direct exposure to the fission particles, they might soon have been seriously injured."

With *Nevada* uninhabitable, her crew, which due to transfers now numbered only 19 officers and 305 enlisted men, transferred to the more lightly contaminated target ship USS *Cortland* (APA-75) on August 18.

On August 19, per Adm. Blandy's orders, the tug *Preserver* towed *Nevada* from Bikini bound for Kwajalein, where they arrived on August 23.

On August 26, *Nevada*'s ship's post office ceased to exist. The next day, a work party went aboard to recover a few items but were aboard only briefly. On August 29, while anchored at A-11 at Kwajalein and her crew aboard *Cortland*, USS *Nevada* was decommissioned. However, Blandy was concerned that ammunition might cook off in the tropic heat, so on October 14 and again on October 26, men went aboard to remove and dump some of the 5-inch and smaller ammunition, the main battery ammo being too heavy to manhandle.

Nevada rested at anchor at Kwajalein until 1947, when she was towed to Pearl Harbor, arriving on March 14, 1947. She was moored, along with *New York*, in East Loch, with large signs posted reading "Danger Keep Off." On July 26, 1948, a secret explosive was placed aboard *Nevada*, and she was towed from Pearl to a point 65 miles southwest of Oahu, where the water was 15,000 feet deep and her radiation would no longer be a threat.

The new secret demolition charges had little effect on the "Cheer Up" ship. Aircraft-launched guided bombs then were unleashed, but they fell short of the resolute *Nevada*. Destroyers advanced, hammering away with their 5-inch guns but causing little damage. The mighty USS *Iowa* unleashed her 16-inch main battery—the kind of ship that *Nevada* had been designed to face, but the venerable battlewagon's armor held against her newer sibling. A trio of light cruisers, *Astoria*, *Pasadena*, and *Springfield*, fired dozens of 6-inch rounds at the veteran battleship, further demolishing her topsides, but she defiantly remained afloat.

Aviators took another turn, firing rockets, striking *Nevada* repeatedly to little avail. For four and a half days, "Old Imperishable," as she had come to be known during World War II, endured beating after beating from aircraft and warships. In all, during the effort to sink *Nevada*, 27 16-inch shells, 113 6-inch shells, and 147 5-inch shells, for a total of 287 rounds, were fired.

Finally, at 1400 on July 31, 1948, just as she had been on December 7, 1941, she was hit by an air-launched torpedo. She began to list to starboard before capsizing and sinking by the stern at 1434.

Fittingly, as the Washington, DC, *Evening Star* reported, after *Nevada* disappeared, *Iowa* "then moved slowly over the spot where the *Nevada* went down 66 miles southwest of Honolulu. The crew in dress whites stood at attention as the brief committal service was read. The epitaph came from Adm. Dewitt C. Ramsey, commander of the Pacific Fleet, who watched from a destroyer escort. Turning to a reporter he said, 'She was a grand old ship.'"

Nevada is about to arrive at Pearl Harbor on May 8, 1946, where she will stay for a few days before departing for Bikini Atoll. For the transit from San Pedro to Pearl Harbor, the ship had a skeleton crew. At Pearl Harbor, an array of military weapons, vehicles, and equipment would be loaded onto the decks; this materiel would be subjected to the atomic blasts, and the effects analyzed in detail. A considerable amount of military equipment is already on the aft part of the main deck in this photo. *National Archives*

In her berth, F-8, at Pearl Harbor, the same berth she occupied at the beginning of the Japanese attack on Pearl Harbor, *Nevada* was extensively photographed, as a record of the ship before the atomic tests. As indicated by the identification card attached to the mount, the photo was taken on May 18, 1946, to document the bucklers, or blast bags, on the number 2 twin 5-inch/38-caliber gun mount. On the roof of the gun shield (as the housing of these gun mounts was called, instead of turrets) is the open hatch and blast hood for the mount captain, with a ring-and-bead sight present above the hatch. The twin 5-inch/38-caliber gun mounts were assigned odd numbers, fore to aft, on the port side of the ship and even numbers on the port side. Hence, mount 2 was the forward one on the port side. *National Archives*

Also taken on May 18 is this view of the left side of the number 2 twin 5-inch/38-caliber gun mount, with the armored hoods and shutters for the pointer's (*front*) and the sight checker's (*rear*) telescopes jutting from the side of the shield. The pointer controlled the elevation of the guns when the mount was under "local," or manual, control, rather than under the control of a gun director. The sight checker was not a regular member of the gun-mount crew; instead, he trained the mount captain, trainer (who controlled the azimuth of the mount under local control), pointer, and sight setter in the use of their equipment and observed the effect of shots through this telescope. *National Archives*

The pointer's and checker's stations in the left front corner of the number 1 twin 5-inch/38-caliber gun mount are viewed in this photo taken on June 3, 1946. The pointer's tractor-type seat is to the right of the identification card. Above and to the front of the seat is the pointer's telescope, partly hidden by plumbing. Near the top of the photo is the checker's telescope, horizontally mounted.

The trainer's station in the number 7 twin 5-inch/38-caliber gun mount, located in the right front of the mount, was photographed on June 3, 1946. At the center of the photo is the trainer's tractor-type seat. The box to the front of the seat is the train indicator-regulator, above which are the train handwheel drive assembly and the trainer's telescope. *National Archives*

Each twin 5-inch/38-caliber gun mount had two projectile hoists, for bringing shells up from the upper handling room, immediately below the mount. The hoists, seen in a photo taken on June 3, 1946, were located in the center of the mount. In the center background, toward the front of the mount, are the fuse setter's and the sight setter's stations. Since the ammunition for the 5-inch guns was two-piece, projectile and powder cartridge, there also were two powder hoists per mount, aft of the projectile hoists. *National Archives*

A projectile and a powder cartridge are on the loading tray of the right gun in the number 8 twin 5-inch/38-caliber gun mount, as photographed on June 6, 1946. The gun is set at high elevation. To the left are the right projectile hoist and, to the rear of the projectiles on the floor, the top of the powder hoist. At the far right are the rammer hydraulic tank and the rammer hydraulic motor. *National Archives*

Immediately below each twin 5-inch/38-caliber gun mount is an upper handling room, where projectiles and powder cartridges are stored in readiness for hoisting them up to the gun mount. This upper handling room was the one for mount 8. *National Archives*

The right-hand rangefinder hood on turret 4 is seen facing forward in a photo dated May 17, 1946. Below the hood is the barbette for turret 3. *National Archives*

The left rangefinder hood on turret 4 also was photographed on May 17. Air- and surface-search radar antennas and other small antennas, *to the upper left*, would remain in place on the ship for the atomic tests. *National Archives*

The trainer's station in turret 3 is the subject of this photo taken on May 17, 1946. The trainer controlled the traverse, or azimuth, of the 14-inch guns when they were under local control. *National Archives*

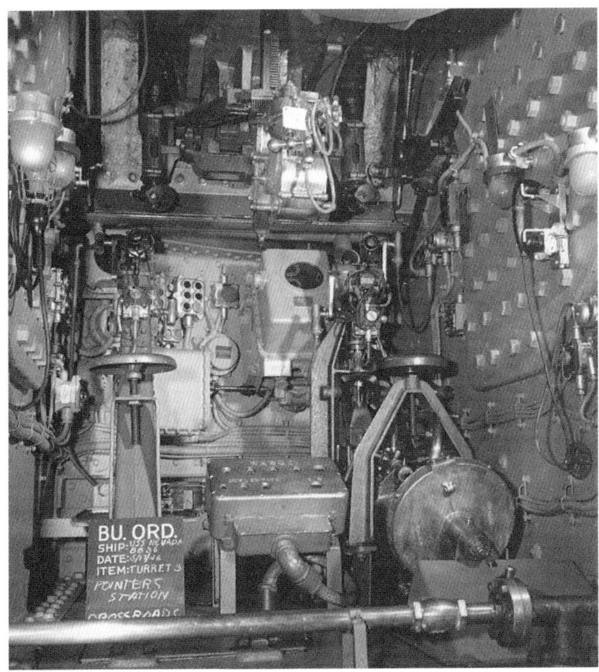

Taken on the same date was this view of the pointer's station in turret 3. From here, the pointer would operate the 14-inch guns' elevation mechanisms during local control. *National Archives*

The following sequence of photos, taken on May 17 and 20, 1946, documents the bucklers, or blast bags, on the 14-inch guns of *Nevada* before the Bikini Atoll atomic tests. Shown here is the underside of the buckler of the right gun of turret 4. *National Archives*

The bottom of the buckler of the center gun of turret 4 is emphasized, with the inner sides of the bucklers of the other two guns also shown. *National Archives*

The bucklers of all three guns of turret 1, as seen from the turret roof facing forward, had networks of overlapping seams. *National Archives*

The open breech of the left 14-inch gun of turret 3 is viewed from the rear. To the rear of the breech is the spanning tray, which holds the projectiles and the powder bags as they are rammed into the chamber. The breechblock swiveled down when open; part of it, with interrupted threads prominent on it, is visible below the breech. At the bottom is the cradle, which was hinged to the rear of the spanning tray. The cradle was used along with the spanning tray to load projectiles only, not powder bags. *National Archives*

Inside turret 4, several 14-inch projectiles and a bag of SPCG powder are laid out for purposes of assessing the effects of atomic blasts on them. The rectangular feature with vertical and horizontal ribs at the center of the photo is a powder hoist door. This door was hinged on the bottom and was opened to allow powder bags to roll down it onto a spanning tray. *National Archives*

Projectiles were stored upright several levels below the turrets in spaces called projectile flats (or, in the case of the identification card in this photo taken below turret 4, shell decks). Through a process called parbuckling, the projectiles were skidded from their storage spots through a system of capstans and ropes to the shell hoists, where they were sent up to the turrets. *National Archives*

In a photo taken in the well below two of the gun breeches of turret 1, the two tubes are projectile hoists. Crewmen called primer men operated in the well below the gun breeches; they were responsible for inserting primers into the firing locks preparatory to firing the guns. *National Archives*

An aerial view of *Nevada* shows her painted orange and prepared for the nuclear tests at Bikini Atoll. The photo predates May 10, 1946, on which date it was cleared for publication; *Nevada* had arrived at Pearl Harbor two days before that date. Various military vehicles to be subjected to the atomic tests are parked on the decks, adjacent to turret 2 and on the afterdeck. *National Archives*

Nevada arrived at Bikini Atoll on May 28, 1946, where preparations for her role in the atomic tests continued. Here, in front of a twin 5-inch/38-caliber dual-purpose gun mount, correspondents are being briefed on military equipment, including several types of small arms and automatic guns, slated to be subjected to atomic blasts. *National Archives*

At anchor in the lagoon at Bikini Atoll, *Nevada* awaits the Operation Crossroads nuclear blasts. The photo was published in newspapers in the United States on June 29, 1946, two days before the first atomic test, code-named Able. "NEVADA 36" is painted in white on the hull just aft of the anchor, and reference marks are painted in white on the bow, as a guide to the ship's draft after the atomic explosions. The ship's frame numbers are painted in white near the top of the hull in increments of ten.

The first atomic bomb used in Operation Crossroads, code-named Able, was a 23-kiloton "Fat Man" weapon, dropped from a B-29 Superfortress and set to air-burst at about 500 feet above the lagoon, on July 1, 1946. Despite the bright-orange paint on the target ship, *Nevada*, the bombardier missed the target by about 2,000 feet. According to the official Navy report of the test, *Nevada* suffered "moderate" damage, with much damage to the more fragile structures on the ship.

The second and last atomic test of Operation Crossroads, code-named Baker, was on the morning of July 25, 1946. This was an underwater explosion, 90 feet below the surface. As seen in this stunning photo, the Baker blast generated a column of water and steam some 2,000 feet in diameter. The shock of the blast and the force of millions of tons of water crashing back down to the surface raised havoc with the test fleet, yet *Nevada* came through the Baker test still afloat. *National Archives*

Two days after the Able detonation, a boarding party was cleared to inspect *Nevada*. In this undated photo, the aircraft crane is still standing but its lower section was severely twisted. Much wreckage litters the aft part of the main deck, including aircraft, vehicles, and even an artillery piece that were being tested for their endurance against an atomic bomb. *Randy Fagan, The Floating Drydock collection*

In a photo taken above the catapult facing forward, wrecked equipment on the deck includes a DUKW amphibious vehicle (*left*) and an artillery piece (*right*). Farther forward on the left, a man in light-colored overalls is inspecting an M36 tank destroyer. The blast mangled the radar and communications equipment on the mast tops. Most of the blast bags on the turrets have been mangled or completely torn off.

In a view off *Nevada*'s port stern, the wracked aircraft crane and the crumpled DUKW are evident. The yardarms were twisted, and one was missing. The down blast of the Able explosion surged down the smokestack of *Nevada*, wrecking her boiler casings.

In August 1946 the Navy ordered that test ships from Operation Crossroads that were still seaworthy be moved to Kwajalein. *Nevada* was seen as the salvage-and-rescue ship USS *Preserver* (ARS-8) was preparing to tow her to Kwajalein. That journey began on August 19. Wreckage and debris had been removed from the decks.

In a companion view to the preceding photo, *Nevada* is viewed from a closer perspective. To the far right is the M36 tank destroyer test vehicle. Stenciled frame numbers in increments of ten are along the upper hull. Although the original US Navy captions for this and the preceding photo indicated that they showed *Nevada* being towed, no tow cables are visible.

This undated photograph of *Nevada* after the Bikini atomic tests may have been taken at the anchorage at Kwajalein. There is no evidence of the damaged ships that littered the lagoon at Bikini. Most of the debris from the atomic blasts had been removed from *Nevada*, although the M36 tank destroyer is still parked on the main deck next to turret 4. *Randy Fagan, The Floating Drydock collection*

After lying in the anchorage at Kwajalein for ten months, the highly radioactive hulk of *Nevada* was towed across the Pacific to Pearl Harbor, where, assisted by tugs, she is seen arriving on June 26, 1947. *National Archives*

A party of Eagle Scouts on a motor launch, touring Pearl Harbor on February 9, 1948, are passing close by the battleship USS *New York* (BB-34), one of the US warships that had been subjected to tests at Bikini Atoll in July 1946. Most eyes seem to be focused on *Nevada*, anchored across the channel. *National Archives*

The decommissioned battleships *New York* (*left*) and *Nevada* are at anchor in Pearl Harbor on June 8, 1948. Like *Nevada*, *New York* was scheduled for destruction at sea the following month. *National Archives*

Declared unsalvageable because she was highly radioactive, *Nevada* was earmarked for sinking in waters 15,000 feet deep, 65 nautical miles southwest of Pearl Harbor. She is departing Pearl Harbor for the last time, on July 26, 1948. *National Archives*

In the last several days of July 1948, US Navy ships and aircraft assaulted *Nevada* with an array of weapons, from gunfire and radar-guided glide bombs to rockets and torpedoes. This exercise was a combination of ordnance tests, weapons practice, and deliberate destruction of the hulk. Here, two waterspouts from hits or near misses have erupted along the starboard side, adjacent to the forward turrets. *National Archives*

A rocket, possibly one of the Tiny Tim air-to-surface antiship rockets used against *Nevada*, has exploded on the starboard hull, amidships; a stream of smoke, as from rocket exhaust, leads diagonally to the explosion. Water geysers from several near misses are seen beyond the aft part of the ship. *National Archives*

Smoke is pouring from the superstructure of *Nevada*; according to the original US Navy text accompanying the photo, it was taken on July 31, 1948, just before she began to sink. *National Archives*

In a photo evidently taken moments from the preceding one, the damage to the superstructure and the above-decks structures of *Nevada* is evident. It was finally two torpedoes, released from Navy torpedo bombers and striking the hull amidships, that sealed *Nevada*'s fate. *National Archives*

Finally, after being hit by two torpedoes, *Nevada* capsized. She is seen moments before sinking, her bulbous bow to the right. Two large holes are visible on her hull. *National Archives*

Only the bulbous bow is still above the waves as *Nevada* goes down, on July 31, 1948. It is the last that was seen of the heroic battleship until an exploration team discovered and photographed her on the floor of the ocean, 65 nautical miles southwest of Oahu, on April 29, 2020. *National Archives*